# THE
# EXTREMELY SUCCESSFUL
# SALESMAN'S CLUB

# THE
# EXTREMELY SUCCESSFUL
# SALESMAN'S CLUB

## US EDITION

## CHRIS MURRAY

The Extremely Successful Salesman's Club

A Lucrum House Book: 9781849144179

First published in Great Britain in 2013 by Lucrum House

Visit the website at *www.TheESSClub.com* or follow on Twitter *@TheESSClub*

*The Extremely Successful Salesman's Club* © Chris Murray 2009

Cover Picture by Simon Tappenden
Lucrum House Books are published by Completely Novel

Design by Christopher Derrick for Unauthorized Media

ISBN 9781849144179

# CONTENTS

The Legend of The Extremely Successful Salesman's Club

To all those who feel that success is waiting just around the corner, but wish someone would show them which corner it is they should turn.

And to SJ, EJ & AC - With all my love

# THE LEGEND OF THE EXTREMELY SUCCESSFUL SALESMAN'S CLUB

Of all the exclusive Victorian Gentleman's clubs, The Extremely Successful Salesman's (ESS) Club was often described as the "*most elite and important of all London clubs.*"

Standing in close proximity to St. James Square, the Club was noted for its magnificent smoking and dining rooms, and extensive library. It was instantly recognisable to the well-informed by the large cochlea shell engraved in the glass above the front door. The cochlea was the symbol of the Club and served as a reminder that all who entered practised the art of deep listening.

From its London inception in 1843, as a dining club for the professional classes of the City, it quickly became a place where the like-minded could share their wisdom, secrets, and methods that had provided them their success.

These "success" lessons were later distilled into the Club's legendary *7 Rules, 5 Truths, and 3 Laws.*

**"...they shall end by becoming prosperous enough to join the Whittington Club, or the ESS Club, or the Gresham Club, or the Travellers' Club....the Club is composed of merchants, bankers, and other gentlemen of known respectability. No candidate is eligible, until he has attained the age of twenty-one years..."**

**An Exploration of London Society – Ishmael Cayton Jones**

Membership was by invitation only, with the weeklong initiation ceremony conducted by the new member's sponsor. A week being the time expected for an inductee to grasp the 7 Rules – the minimum expected understanding – in full. After proving himself over a twelve-month period, the Apprentice was considered for the position of Neophyte, and then could move toward becoming a Journeyman.

*The 5 Truths and 3 Laws* were rites of passage in themselves, only revealed to those who had proven themselves to be truly worthy, and were delivered with the award of a gold, and then a platinum membership.

As a physical entity, the Club disappeared sometime after the First World War. However, the rules, laws, and truths continued under a variety of different guises, passed from generation to generation.

There are those, who say that the society still exists, controlling and manipulating international trade with their vast network of contacts and combined knowledge. And that they continue to put the ancient secrets of the Club to the very use they were intended – *making those who know them extremely successful.*

# CHAPTER 1
## A Rather Beguiling Invitation

*Dear Simeon,*

I am well aware that the last few years have not been easy for you or your family and would like to offer my sincerest sympathies following the sudden passing of your father. With this in mind, I have decided to offer you a chance to improve your fortunes to the best of my ability.

It is well-known that a man can only be as successful as the network of associates to which he belongs. Therefore, I would like to make you a unique offer, which if you do not accept at once, will unfortunately be beyond my influence to present to you again.

Since you have recently celebrated your twenty-first birthday, I am able to sponsor your induction to an establishment over which

I hold some small influence. It is simply known as The Extremely Successful Salesman's Club.

Before you make your decision, I need to make you aware that there is an incredibly strict apprenticeship, which among other tasks, includes the absorption of seven critical rules.

If, after accompanying me for a full week in London, we discover that you are able to abide by these rules and are accepted by the inner chamber of the Club, then I can promise you that your life will never be quite the same.

It would not be untrue to say this purposefully private Club, has enabled many men, from a variety of backgrounds to become extremely successful, and in turn, fabulously wealthy.

It is this opportunity that I wish to share with you.

Having no children of my own, I have been allowed to extend the invitation of a trial membership to you, Simeon, my only nephew.

Do not back away from this through a fear of possibility or opportunity, as so many do. Instead, embrace it wholeheartedly, and take your first steps towards an incredibly prosperous life.

I will be waiting for you in the Club's dining room at eight on the evening of the fourth. If you decide that you will not be joining me, I will understand, and we shall never mention this again.

However, as you may recall, I do so hate to eat alone.

Best Regards,

*Barnabas Kreuz*

# CHAPTER 2
## A Most Vexing Decision

AFTER RECEIVING THE INVITATION from his uncle, Simeon had made all the necessary arrangements and on the evening of the fourth, in a rather apprehensive mood, was dropped by cab close to the central London address.

Carrying a small case with one hand, and holding a business card high in the other, he strolled briskly in the warmth of the late summer air, trying to get a sense of the direction in which the house numbers ran around the square.

This curious little card had accompanied the invitation from his uncle. It was inscribed with the St. James' address on one side and a sketch of what appeared to be a small whirlpool on the reverse. He counted down from the last building showing a visible street number, until arriving at his destination.

Walking through the small gate and up the large stone steps

towards the foreboding black-paneled door, he noticed the same whirlpool design engraved in the semi-circular window above.

With one last deep breath to steady himself, he knocked.

As the door opened, Simeon felt dizzy and slightly nauseous, a feeling he would later contribute to nerves. The tall, balding, white-gloved man in the doorway gazed just above Simeon's head.

"May I help you?"

"I am here to meet with my uncle Barnabas, Barnabas Kreuz…"

His explanation was cut short by a booming voice from within.

"He's with me, Jenkins. This is my nephew. I'll look after him from here."

Through the door, Simeon could see a great bear of a man bounding across the mosaic-tiled floor. He was exquisitely dressed and sported a wide moustache, which framed his beaming smile.

"Uncle Barnabas!"

"Hello, my boy. Well, let him in, Jenkins. Come on. Poor boy can't get started from out there."

Jenkins nodded, and indicated to a small desk just inside the door.

"Certainly, Sir. The gentleman will, of course, be required to sign the visitor's book during his stay."

"Quite so. Quite right. Come on, my boy, let's make this legal and above board."

Simeon stepped into the vast entrance hall and looked up to the ceiling, which rose through two floors above them. The area was framed by a number of internal balconies. To his left was a manned cloakroom, and ahead a pair of large solid doors.

Barnabas took Simeon's coat, while enquiring about the journey and then, once pleasantries were over, he placed a hand on either side of the young man's shoulders, his smile dropping slightly.

"It is fabulous to see you and I am delighted that you accepted my invitation. I truly am. However, forgive me for a moment, while I take a more somber tone. You see, our time together is limited and this undertaking is of a most serious nature. The information I will be sharing with you throughout this week must remain for your ears only. Do you understand?"

"I do."

"Good, good. In my letter, I promised you an opportunity for success and wealth. However, these next few days act only as a guide of the routes and roads to be taken. If the man taking the quest is not up to this task, then simply understanding these directions will not suffice."

"Thank you, Uncle. I have been warned. Let's get started."

"One moment. Take your time, young man. I have a number of questions to ask you." Barnabas pointed to the wall behind him saying, "You should only step through this next set of doors if you genuinely wish for your life to change. Please listen to these words, as I ask you, most earnestly. Do you wish to become wealthier than you can currently comprehend, with success you cannot yet possibly dream of?"

"Yes, I do – who wouldn't? Why would you ask?"

Barnabas stared as if strangely possessed, his voice showing signs of impatience.

"Because it's so vitally important, that's why! I need you to focus. Imagine in your mind's eye your personal interpretation of wealth."

Simeon raised his brow, stared slightly to the right and grinned.

"I have it."

Barnabas tapped two fingers on the top of the young man's head.

"You hardly had time to visualize anything at all. Take your time, concentrate hard, and then ask yourself, are you ready to start the journey that will take you there?"

Simeon took a deep, slightly-agitated breath, closed his eyes, and thought hard on his uncle's request.

"Yes. I truly am."

"Do you want to join the ranks of the extremely successful?"

"Of course I do, without doubt!"

"Do you understand that only a small number of men have ever been invited to join this Club, and fewer still ever take permanent residence in the greater society beyond these doors?"

"I do now."

"And yet you still wish to continue?"

"Yes, of course. Whatever else you have to warn me of, Uncle, shall we just assume that I accept and we can move on."

"Assumption is not in my nature, dear boy. Listen to me carefully. One way or another your life is about to change! Few people hear these words when offered, but I will share them anyway, and you will no doubt hear me say them again and again. Your life *will* change! You don't realize it yet, but you are currently in a fairly enviable position of ignorance."

"Thank you very much, I'm sure. Ignorant and enviable. What a perfectly delightful combination."

"Not very often, but on this occasion, yes. Each and every person, who stood at this threshold spent some time afterwards wishing they had turned away. Once you and I lift the lid on Pandora's box, it will always be open. You will not be able to unlearn what you have learnt."

"You are warning me of the consequences of my own success?"

"Or the opposite. There have been those who walked through these doors unwilling to rise to the challenge. They now spend their lives constantly aware of what could have been theirs, knowing that their own weaknesses keep them from true happiness. Its propinquity an unremitting reminder of their failure. If that is to be your destiny, then I'm afraid your future holds nothing but anger and bitterness"

Simeon swallowed hard, the cheerfulness draining from his features.

"So I ask you, before you go any further, do you still wish to accept my invitation to join The Extremely Successful Salesman's Club?"

A slight hesitation, and then Simeon answered,

"Yes!"

Barnabas produced a bright, golden key attached by a short chain to the inside of his jacket. Simeon could hear the echoes in the space beyond where they stood, as the key turned in the lock. Barnabas threw open the large, double doors, signaling for his nephew to walk through them.

Ahead of them was a corridor of around twenty feet in length. The floor paved with highly-polished, black-and-white diamonds, bordered by portraits of austere men, who looked down on the pair as they walked past like discontented chess pieces watching over a narrow marble board.

Simeon suddenly felt as though he had not been ready for this at all.

# CHAPTER 3
## The Secret Place of Thunder

THEY MADE THEIR WAY TOWARDS the single, brown, leather-padded door at the other end of the corridor. Their clacking steps echoing all around them, and reverberating up to the high, white ceiling above.

As Barnabas stopped, key in hand and brow raised, his eyes gestured to the room beyond the door.

Simeon nodded. His uncle grinned, took a deep breath, and pushed the door inward.

The round windowless room ahead of them was empty but for a three-legged table standing over a mural of a mariner's star.

An identical door perfectly mirrored the one from which they had just entered.

Simeon looked up and noticed that there was an inscription

written around the wall just beneath the cornice:

*"Thou calledst in trouble, and I delivered thee; I answered thee in the secret place of thunder."*

As Simeon walked across to the table, he heard the heavy door shut hard behind him.

Desperate for something to say to break the silence, he nodded towards the other door.

"Where does that one lead?"

"That is a completely different set of golden keys altogether. One room at a time, my boy, one room at a time."

His uncle paced around the outside edge of the room, rocked back on his heels, and raised his arm towards the table.

"I believe there is an envelope addressed to you. Kindly open it."

Simeon moved closer as instructed, an envelope sat on top of a thick, ancient book. The corners of its heavy cover were dark and tatty, the edges of its inner pages thick and jagged.

"This is an old book."

"One of the oldest."

"Why is it kept in here, all locked up?"

"My boy, that book is more than a thousand years old. It was brought to London after the third crusade. And then passed down through generations of one of England's most well-known families. That book contains the true secrets of success. The very foundations of this entire establishment." Barnabas smiled a respectful smile. "You know, after all this time, we still haven't translated it all. To this day, it continues to keep some secrets from us, deep within its ancient pages."

Simeon looked skeptical.

"You're telling me that this esteemed Club bases its techniques on an untranslatable, thousand-year-old book?"

Barnabas looked genuinely aggrieved.

"There are no mere techniques here. This book contains principles, my boy. True undisputable principles. You won't find fashionable ideas or parlor tricks disguised as wisdom in this mighty tome. Techniques, young man, are to be learned and discarded. Principles are to be understood and absorbed. Principles are what you build your life around. No. What we have here is the lost Eighth Book."

"I'm sorry. Is that supposed to mean something to me?"

"Ha, my apologies, dear boy. Probably not, but you are more than likely aware of the rest of its family. Over two thousand years ago, select members of the intelligentsia put together eight pieces of literature. Over the centuries they were largely forgotten as actual physical objects, but you've no doubt heard them referred to as The Seven Pillars."

"The Seven Pillars of Wisdom? You're saying that they were once physical books?"

"Of course, absolutely! The Book of Power, The Book of Knowledge, the Books of Understanding and Counsel, followed by Prudence, Discretion, and Sound Judgement. But this book, the book you see before you here, this is the Eighth Book. This is the complete collection, an intense distillation of the other seven."

He placed his hand gently on the ancient tanned cover, his face beaming, his voice lowered to a reverent hush,

"This, Simeon, is The Book of Success."

Simeon's face showed a mixture of doubt and disbelief.

"So this is my challenge. I am to read and understand this long-lost Eighth Book of Wisdom?"

Barnabas boomed a laugh.

"Good God no! That would take you forever. Probably bore you to death before that. No, you must read the rather shorter letter, placed on top of the book, which I believe you will find is addressed to you."

The young man's nervous fingers found a small opening above the wax, ripped through the top, and unfolded the paper within.

Barnabas smiled at Simeon's bewildered expression.

"What do you see?"

"It states my name and that this, or rather, that these, are the Seven Rules of The Extremely Successful Salesman's Club. Then, there is a list of random statements. It says I must learn these rules. I must live them and make them work for me as they have done for the chosen few before me. I must follow the path of those, who have gone before me and spend my time piecing together the letters of the secret word of success. The word that means all things."

"You're frowning?"

"Well, these statements don't seem to make any sense. How am I supposed to follow rules that I can't make head nor tail of? And how can a single word mean all things?"

"That, my boy, is precisely what I'm here for. Intrigued?"

"Confused!"

There was a silence, and then Barnabas raised his hands.

"Well that's a start, I suppose. Come, we should eat. You must be famished – and no one should ever be confused and hungry at the same time, eh?"

# CHAPTER 4
## The First Rule: Adopt the Positive

A S THEY SETTLED DOWN FOR DINNER, Barnabas motioned towards the back of the room with his hand.

"Do you see that large lobster tank over there?"

Simeon turned to see a large rectangular aquarium in the corner of the room

"Oh yes. I don't know how I missed that on the way in."

"Ha! We shall deal with your limited powers of observation at a later date, my boy. For now just watch how they interact will you."

Simeon unfolded the large white napkin resting across his plate, and turned to watch as the lobsters clawed their way onto each other's backs, making tall columns before toppling backwards and joining the other inhabitants on the base of the tank. He became captivated by this strangely hypnotic display, quickly realizing that the collapse was due to the majority pulling the top lobster back down amongst them.

He turned back to his uncle, smiling.

"How strange. Those lobsters could easily climb out of the tank. There seems to be no lid or impediment to their escape. Yet each time one gets near to the top, the rest pull him right back to the bottom."

"Well spotted," said Barnabas. "Bizarre. Is it not?"

They both watched a little longer before he gestured with an open hand towards a newly emerging tower of lobsters.

"You know, Simeon, I see lobsters pretty much everywhere."

"I'm sorry?"

Barnabas dabbed the side of his mouth and laughed.

"Don't worry. I'm not suffering from some form of crustacean-based madness. I'm not delusional. What I mean is this. I recognize lobster-like qualities in the way people interact. That tank is simply a reflection of how the human race regularly treat one another. Most don't even know they're doing it. It just appears to be the way the human race functions."

"To climb up and pull down?"

"Ha, well in a way I suppose. Ever noticed how others react when you get a chance to better yourself? How they seem to delight in pointing out why the opportunity might be beyond your capabilities? Above your station in life or just so far out of reach it would be pointless to even try for? They seem to mean well, don't they? Have your best interests at heart? They'll be convincing and sincere, but all they are actually doing is passing on their personal fears and superstitions regarding life outside of their own private lobster tank."

Simeon nodded, placing his knife and fork neatly at the side of his plate.

"I have to say there has been no shortage of people, who advised me to set my aspirations at a level beneath my abilities. Even more who mocked my personal self-beliefs. Maybe I'm fooling myself, but I always felt there must be a way to achieve my hopes and dreams, make my family proud."

"And you shall, young man. You shall! And by adopting this first rule, *you will!*"

Simeon was carefully flattening his newly-acquired letter on the table in front of him.

"So what does *adopt the positive* actually mean?"

Barnabas put his hand on Simeon's elbow and leant in.

"It means you fill your life with positive people, positive conversation, and positive literature. It means you politely ignore naysayers, understanding that everything you do has a consequence. The subject matter you decide to read or not read, believe or not believe, the words you say or don't say, wherever you decide to go or not to go. These are your choices every day and they are decisions of vast importance. Pity the naysayers, if you wish, but do so remembering you have better things to spend your time on than trying to convert those who fear success."

"Pity them. Ignore them. That all sounds rather uncharitable."

"No. Not really. Just realistic."

"And who would fear success?"

"Pretty much everyone."

"Nonsense. I can't subscribe to that. Who wouldn't want to be rich beyond their wildest dreams?"

"Come now. I saw the fear in your eyes when we discussed failure in the lobby. How many people would actually make the most of success if the chance came, eh? Allowing yourself to be a conduit for opportunity requires a brand new outlook on life. Lady fortune cannot enter a locked door, you know. And contrary to that well-known saying, she has rarely been known to knock."

"So how do I make sure she comes somewhere near my door then?"

"Ha, straight to it, eh? Good for you, good for you. Well, you do so by keeping your head up and your eyes open. You listen. You become aware. You recognize coincidence and you notice the gaps that so many others miss."

"Gaps? I can assure you, Uncle. There's nothing out there being missed. Every way of making a living is already being taken advantage of by someone."

"Do you think so?"

"I know so."

"You know so do you? My dear boy, you really need to adopt this rule, you really do. If you're not ready to receive opportunity, it'll walk right past you. Carry on believing that every piece of fortune is already spoken for if you want, but while you and your friends are out there looking at your feet wishing life was easier, those destined to be successful can see chances for greatness everywhere right in front of them."

"Why? How is it that they can see what I cannot?"

"Because they're looking, because they're receptive, because they're not being dismissive or negative, because they're eagerly waiting for life to show them the next big clue, the next sign to set them on a road to greater riches and success."

"So you believe that adopting this positive attitude is the magic ingredient to success?"

"No. I do not. But it's where everything starts. Success would be a fairly boring and uninspiring dish if anybody could create it with a single ingredient, however difficult that ingredient was to find. No, success has several layers to its pallet. This is just the beginning."

"Then how should I begin to develop this mindset? How do I *adopt the positive*?"

"Quite simply actually. You just need to start by understanding where you currently are. The fact that you wish to become extremely successful must mean that you currently do not see yourself as such. Therefore, you need to change. The question you should be asking is what do *you* need to become? What kind of a man attracts success?"

"Is that the first rule? Putting my mind to what I should like to become?"

"No. It's just the easiest bit. Disciplining yourself to block out negative thoughts and unhelpful noise is a large part of Rule Number One. Your focus is your reality. Whichever way you are facing is the way you will end up heading."

This conversation was starting to unnerve Simeon. He was not seeking to change himself, just his predicament. And he was quite sure that he liked himself just as he was.

"How much do you think *I* need to change then, Uncle?"

Barnabas realized that some level of comfort was required.

"Consider this, my boy. Would anyone, other than a fool, follow the same instructions time after time, do the same thing over and over again, and expect different results on each occasion?"

Barnabas paused, waiting for Simeon's response.

"Well, I suppose if you walk the same path every day, you will always end up at the same place. That would be obvious."

"Quite so. Quite right. And yet human beings, who dream of becoming more successful often fool themselves into believing that it can happen without changing a single thing about themselves. They believe that success is some mysterious external factor that will just sort itself out while they sleep. The truth, Simeon, is that we make *ourselves* successful. We create our own luck by ensuring that we change into the people we wish to become."

He paused, as if trying to catch a memory before continuing, and said, "Trust me. If you do not decide where you are heading, and refuse to take the appropriate action, you will end up being shaped into what others would have you become. Then any change will not be made for your benefit but for theirs. People submit too easily to change from others. And yet, for some reason, whenever they consider changing themselves, the focus is always on what they are giving up, never what they are about to gain. Answer me this. What is the alternative to self-improvement?"

"Staying the same?"

"Staying the same! Precisely! Improve yourself or do not. Your choice. Your responsibility. Everything you desire is always just outside your comfort zone, dear boy. If it wasn't you would already possess it, would you not?"

"I suppose so."

Barnabas smiled. He recognized the light that was starting to sparkle in Simeon's eyes.

"Good. Now let us further translate the meaning within your letter. There is an old line that I'm rather fond of, which is *nobody ever kicked a dog wagging its tail.* I think that sums up this first rule pretty well too, don't you think?"

"Does it? I have no idea."

"Ha. No. Of course you don't. Forgive me. I'm really not very good at this. Listen, selling anything to anyone is all about an exchange of…"

"Money?"

"Ha! We really do have a lot of work to do with you don't we? No, no, no. Money comes in a little later. It's actually all about an exchange of feelings."

"Feelings?"

"Yes. If I can make you feel the same way that I feel about my product or service we'll have a meaningful conversation about it and how it can help. The trouble is that most sales people don't feel anything. Nothing at all."

"In what way?"

"They've never given any thought to how they help people with what they're selling. Therefore, they don't feel anything for it. They just have a vague sense that it's what they have to sell to make money for themselves or to keep their jobs."

"But salesmen are there to sell. That's their role."

"From your side of the table, maybe. From the prospect's side the view is slightly different. You are either trying to help or you're wasting his time."

"So tell me, Uncle. How does this first rule help *me*?" Simeon waved his fingers in front of his face like a magician. "How do I learn this exchanging, mind-trick thing?"

"There are no tricks, no magic. I've already told you that. If you wish to adopt the positive you must learn how you truly help people with the things that you sell. Once you are aware of that vital piece of information every demonstration, every presentation, every transaction will be delivered with a light shining from your heart. From your heart will shine a beacon that tells all prospects you can truly help and that that is your sole purpose for being there."

Simeon sat back in his chair and breathed out hard. He wasn't sure how his products or service had ever really helped anyone. It came as a bit of a shock to realize he really had no idea at all.

# CHAPTER 5
## The Simple Clarification of the Cochlea

SIMEON ATE IN SILENCE PONDERING his uncle's words. When the plates were cleared, Barnabas produced a leather-bound book with the, now familiar, whirlpool embossed in silver upon the cover.

"Here, this is your personal club journal."

Barnabas smiled as Simeon flicked through the empty pages, looking for some form of content, but the sheets inside were blank. Closing the book he indicated to the cover.

"I appear to be seeing this insignia everywhere. Above the door. On your personal card. And now here."

"Of course you do. That, my boy, is a snail's shell."

"The shell of a snail?"

"Yes. Why not?"

"Actually, Uncle, the more obvious question is, why?"

"Ah, apologies, an explanation is required. You will find there are groups all over London with emblems such as ours. The Mercers have engraved the head of a maiden into buildings all across the city. Likewise, you won't have to look too far to see a winged horse, a griffin, or a lamb with a flag. They all represent a society or institution of some description and they all nestle into the very fabric of the capital's architecture, without the common man being any the wiser."

"So some lucky devil gets the mighty griffin, and we end up with a snail's shell. We appear to have the poorer deal, don't you think?"

Barnabas looked quite put out.

"It's not just any shell, my boy. This is *the* snail's shell."

"Oh, *the* snail's shell." Simeon looked less than impressed

"Yes. The cochlea, which as you quite clearly are not aware, also happens to be the exact shape of the inner ear. It was adopted as our symbol as a reminder that selling is about listening, above all things. If you find you are talking more than your prospective client, then you do not represent this Club."

Barnabas pointed to his ears and then his mouth saying,

"Two of these and one of these and they should be used as such. Two ears should be used twice as much as a single mouth, don't you think? So there you have it. That snail is our mark. You can recognize us by our lapel badges, our journals, and our business cards."

"I would never have realized."

"You're not supposed to. What's the point of having secrets if everyone already knows them, eh?"

"So what secrets should I keep in my club journal?"

"Just your own. Over the course of our time together, I will require you to keep a record of our conversations. Keeping a record is crucial. *Vital*."

"Don't worry, Uncle. There is no need for me to make notes. I have a fabulous memory."

"That may be so, but experience has proven to me that if not recorded, if not written down and documented, these precious lessons will more than likely catch the wind like a feather, and linger for a short time in front of your eyes, before leaving forever on the faintest of breezes never to be seen again. I implore you to trust me when I say that even if you never read the words you've written again, your fabulous filing system of a brain will have put them away. It will recognize their importance because you wrote them down, and treasure them. Your brain will keep them somewhere safely noted, until you seek to retrieve them. All due to the simple act of putting pen to paper. The human brain is truly extraordinary is it not, hmm?"

"If you say so, but," Simeon looked slightly uncomfortable, "I'm afraid I'm not much of a writer."

"It matters not. Simply write each entry, as if writing a letter to yourself. Doing so will enable the brain to completely absorb the words, as if they were instructions directly to your subconscious."

Simeon glanced through the empty pages then placed the book by his side.

"What shall I write about this evening?"

"What would you like to write?"

"I don't know. How *do* you start one of these things?"

"It's the same as eating an elephant, really. You start at the beginning, in a place of comfort, and then take it one piece at a time!"

"Eating an elephant?"

"Yes. You'll find many things look big and daunting when you don't know how to approach them. Just start at the beginning and see how it goes."

Simeon smiled and took another sip of wine, as Barnabas continued.

"Let me give you an exercise to start you off. Take thirty or so minutes this evening and make copious notes, absolutely everything that comes to mind. See if you can work out why your current customers buy from you, and which elements of the results of your product they find truly valuable. How was it that you helped them? That, my boy, is the first conundrum to invest a little time on."

Simeon fumbled for the book, turned to the first page, and started to write feverishly across the page.

"Steady there, my dear boy. Make sure you can read it later. Few ever found enlightenment in haste, and nobody will ever discover it in gibberish."

Simeon looked up and smiled, took a breath, and finished writing the task his uncle had assigned to him.

"As a final point, no one else needs to read this journal and I will certainly not be checking whether you are doing as I have asked, at any stage of our time together. Write freely and honestly, include the smallest or largest detail. It makes no difference to anyone but you. This is your life, which is to be improved. No one else's."

"I will, Uncle. You have my word."

Barnabas smiled a tired, knowing smile.

"I need no assurance, my boy. You must make the commitment only to yourself. On every page, you must express yourself in whichever way your emotions take you. Ensure you come back to it often. Write it in words that will help you keep every promise. Speaking of words, let us unlock the final mystery of the night before we move through shall we? What do you make of this secret word, which your paper instructs us to expose?"

Simeon picked up the letter once more.

"It says that I must follow the path of those, who have gone before me, and spend my time piecing together the letters of the secret word of success. The word that means all things."

Simeon turned to his uncle with a look of mocking disbelief.

"Well, I still don't see how that can be. All things? *Really?* Tell me then. What is this fabulous word?"

Barnabas leant back in his chair and smiled.

"After all you have seen so far this evening, all the wonders to which you have been introduced, your reaction remains one of casual disregard for the things you do not understand, mixed with an expectation that the most secret of secrets should suddenly be revealed to you without any personal effort?"

"No, not at all. It was just that I thought you were going to share it with me. Discuss it over brandy, and save us all a bit of time."

"Why? Do you have somewhere else to go?"

"No. Of course not. I have dedicated the week to my efforts here at the Club."

"Well, then, let us learn things in the time they will take to learn shall we."

"You misunderstand me, Uncle. I was…"

"Oh don't upset yourself, lad, I was filled with similar levels of eagerness at one time, you know. Come, back to the puzzle. The letter states that you must follow the path of those who have gone before, and piece together some letters does it not?"

"It does."

"Well, did you know that much of London was either designed or built by members of this very Club?"

"Those who went before?"

"Precisely. And if you knew exactly where to look, you would discover messages and signs sewn into the very walls of some of her most famous monuments and buildings."

"Messages and signs? Regarding the word?"

"In certain places. Others denote directions to private libraries or secret meeting places. Some are just single letters, serving as a trail of breadcrumbs scattered through the largest city on earth. Intriguing and fascinating don't you think?"

"So if I found the right letters, in the right order, I could discover the word?"

"You could."

Simeon's view that this was probably just a waste of time for both men was not hidden from his features.

"But it's like some silly child's game. What would be the point? Why not just *give* me the word?"

"How about because it might be fun?"

"*Fun?*"

"Yes. Why not?"

Simeon gave a little smile. "Of course," he thought. "This might be a little test," and so responded accordingly.

"Uncle, if I could be employing my time more effectively than playing this game, I would like to do so."

"No. There is nothing more important than the word. It may seem pointless to you, but the task is what it is. Why don't we start now? There is actually a letter in this very dining room."

Simeon studied the room, looking at the walls, windows, and ceiling. Nothing.

Barnabas laughed and slapped both palms onto the table. Simeon's face, however, did not portray a man having fun.

"I told you we would deal with your limited powers of observation did I not? Take another look at the lobster tank."

Simeon glared at the tank which, apart from the water and lobsters, was completely empty. The wrought iron stand below was plain and gray. What on earth was he looking for?

Barnabas raised his hand and pointed to the stand, drawing a symbol in the air with his finger.

"Take a good look at the intricate iron work at the front. Remember you are looking for a letter."

Simeon followed his uncle's finger, as it etched out a letter in the space before him. He rather surprised himself with the sense of delight that he felt, as it suddenly came into view.

"I see it. I can see it. It's the letter $N$. There is a capital $N$ making up the whole of the stand."

"Well done, you. There we go. You have your first letter. Make a note of it. We shall have a tougher task of finding the remaining six I can assure you."

Simeon recorded the letter on the inside cover of his journal.

"I have it safe. What now?"

"Now? Well, I think you deserve that brandy now, my boy. Let me introduce you to the rest of this year's hopefuls. A selection of young men, who have just had the same conversation with their own sponsors, are waiting in the games room for us. I think it's time we met the next generation of successful salesmen over a fabulously old Cognac. Don't you?"

*Journal Entry*
*Sunday, 4th September 1887*

This evening, I have seen and heard many things that can change my life, if adopted one by one. But hearing them all together has been quite overwhelming.

I really have no idea how they should be documented, or the order in which they should be recognized.

The first rule states that if I am to become successful, I must embrace a positive attitude. This at first appears incredibly simple to understand and embrace, but once fully considered, it turns into something remarkably intricate.

For instance, I realize, now, that the company I have kept, in the past, has been more to do with my comfort, rather than my happiness.

Of course, my friends, my very good friends, are not people who I will ever abandon or ignore. On the contrary, they should be cherished.

But there is another group. A large company of acquaintances, with whom I simply exist. I feel important in their presence simply because none of them challenge my intellect, or make me feel that I should, or could, be doing better for myself than I already am.

Tonight, I have met like-minded gentlemen, of a similar age to myself, who compete in an arena I had previously avoided. I was afraid that I would look small and insignificant in comparison to them if I tried to compete with them.

In the past, I have plied my trade and foolishly bragged only to those, who I might easily impress. I never pushed myself through the discomfort, of an opportunity, where stretching into its challenge could help me grow, even in defeat.

I have been like a mediocre concert pianist playing in front of a tone-deaf family, who applaud out of duty rather than for accomplishment.

But now, this night, I have met men, who believe they could be giants. They have such a positive attitude towards their future, coupled with a realistic plan of achievement, that I find myself filled with a new energy and purpose.

No longer will I measure myself against competitors, who don't even know that a race is being run. From now on, I will measure myself against the man in front of me. I will measure myself against a new personal best, achieving my next ambitious goal.

Success does not judge one man for being worthy above another. Success doesn't choose you because of your family name or existing wealth.

Success is taken by the man, who has made himself ready for its arrival. And although I am not there yet, I have come to this place to become such a man.

I have set my mind to make sure I am prepared to accept success, whatever the trials ahead, whatever the work required.

I now know that success can not choose me. It is waiting on a path that I must walk. In truth, it waits there for everyone.

Many do not know where the path begins. Some search for a shortcut to the end. But the majority of the world does not even realize there is a path there at all.

I have been shown the start of that path and I am ready.
I have never been so excited by anything in my entire life.
I have adopted the positive.

# CHAPTER 6
## The Second Rule: Embrace the Fundamentals

A FTER A REMARKABLY DEEP night's sleep, Simeon took a light breakfast and headed off. He had agreed to meet Barnabas early that morning by the entrance to the market.

On arrival, his uncle, rather unsettlingly, began with an immediate warning.

"Today is a tough old day, my boy. Rule Number Two is undoubtedly the most difficult of all the rules for a beginner to grasp. Bear with it, though. This is the foundation upon which everything else is built. Now, do I have your full attention?"

Simeon, who had turned to inspect some fruit, nodded reluctantly. Barnabas raised an eyebrow and continued.

"Yesterday, apart from explaining the first rule, we also discussed one of the most important parts of the sales process. Discovering how we help people with our product or service. The deep understanding of that concept is incredibly important for Rule Number Two. Do you have the title?"

"It simply says *embrace the fundamentals*."

"Quite so. Quite right. Embrace the fundamentals. And that is why we have come here. In order for me to explain them to you."

Simeon purchased an apple, bit into it, and turned on his heels with a proud glint in his eye.

"Surely the fundamental requirement for a great salesman is being able to speak with confidence." Simeon smiled a self-satisfied smile. "You know, from an early age people have said that I had the gift of the gab, and that becoming a salesman was what I was born to be. Everybody says so."

"Really? Was that what they said? So you can speak, can you? Well, that's going to stand you out from the rest of the crowd, isn't it? No. Sorry, my boy. The ability to speak does not a salesman make."

"But people adore a bit of confidence, don't they? If you've got the right personality you can sell anything. Customers are desperate for someone who can communicate with them."

"Desperate are they? Desperate for you to communicate what? The thing you want to sell *at* them? You think that's what wins them over? Being spoken *at?* Oh yes, everyone loves a bit of that don't they? No, I'm afraid your overconfidence, as with most young men who dream of becoming successful, can quite quickly become the Achilles' heel of your continued mediocrity."

"Well, so says you. How then do you explain my recent successes?"

Barnabas rubbed his chin.

"Well, at the risk of sounding a bit harsh…I think we can safely say that your recent successes could have just as easily been achieved by a mute monkey in a tiny business suit, holding up a written explanation of whatever it was the monkey was attempting to sell."

"I beg your pardon."

Barnabas raised his voice as if talking to someone slightly deaf.

"I said, you probably had little more effect than a written advertisement gripped by a mute monkey in a tiny, little business suit."

Simeon was flabbergasted. Barnabas, however, just lowered his voice again and continued.

"I'd imagine the customers so desperately required your services that they were probably going to buy no matter what happened. Your major contribution to the whole affair was to keep out of the way long enough for them to pay for it."

"I think calling your comments harsh is a bit of an understatement. I believe you will find, Uncle, that I had an awful lot to do with each and every one of those transactions."

"Really? Are you sure? Did you sell to them or did you simply facilitate their buying *from* you, hmm? Very different scenarios, my boy, very different indeed. But listen, you can't know what you don't know. Put your trust in me on this point. Stop sulking and let us begin the work of improving your future prospects shall we?"

Barnabas put his arm across Simeon's shoulders and led him towards more stalls.

"Remember this. We are always looking for problems to solve, and to solve problems we need to be ready for clues. And you will never be in the receiving frame of mind if you – never – shut-up!"

He highlighted each word by driving his stick into the cobbles.

"So I'm wrong, again."

"No. Not completely. But I shall not waste any of our brief time together flattering your ego, as others have done before, with all this nonsense about skills and talents that do not help, or worse, that you do not actually possess."

"So then, enlighten me, Uncle. What are these fabulous fundamentals?"

"Yes, indeed. Quite right. Quite so. Always moving forward. Simply put, they concentrate on why anyone would want to talk to us in the first place. And they concentrate on enabling us to explain to our customers how we can help them."

"Well, that doesn't sound too difficult. Where do we start?"

"Rather unsurprisingly," Barnabas smiled and said, "at the beginning."

He then stretched out his hands, indicating that Simeon should look around the entire marketplace.

"If you wish to sell to anyone you must earn the right to do so. Without taking this first step, nothing meaningful will ever happen. Take a look around you, my boy. It may appear that everyone is making money, but each day stalls close, and traders are replaced, because if you cannot entice the customers today, there may be no stall tomorrow."

For a short time, they listened together as the traders called to passing customers. Some were incredibly loud, others extraordinarily cheeky, all of them confident and believable.

As they strolled between the stalls, Barnabas continued.

"It has been my experience that around half of those offering a product or service, in every line of business, are quite utterly useless. Some of them actually bordering on criminal. The remainder are split between two camps, the acceptable and the exceptional. Unfortunately for the average man on the street, it is incredibly difficult to recognize which is which. Most of what's on offer seems rather similar, with prices that, at first glance, appear to be comparable. Therefore, the only thing, which really sets suppliers apart in the prospect's eye, is the perception of how each vendor may be able to aid them reach their desired outcome. Who has the expertise to truly help them and how much can we trust them to deliver what they promise?"

Barnabas stopped and leant against his stick. "Did you complete last night's exercises on how you help people?"

"Yes. To the letter."

"Fabulous. Well, here is a question for you then. That chap over there, buying a spade from the iron mongers stall, what do you think he wants?"

Simeon pulled a face to indicate how stupid he felt answering such an obvious question.

"A spade?"

"Does he? Does he really want a spade?"

"Well, if he doesn't want a spade that stall holder must be the best salesman in the entire market, because he is just about to sell him one."

Barnabas laughed.

"Come along. Nobody just wants a spade. It's hardly an attractive trinket. Think deeper. What does he want to do with it?"

"Maybe he wants to dig a hole."

"Quite so. Quite right. He may very well wish to dig himself a hole. So then, he doesn't really want a spade. What he wants is the hole does he not?"

"But he needs the spade."

"Yes. But only because he wants a hole. Without the requirement for a hole, there would be no need to buy the spade."

"Fair enough. I can understand that thought process working for something like a spade, but it hardly applies to many other things."

"Do you think so? When the butcher sells a side of beef, did the customer just want to possess a piece of dead bull?"

"No. Clearly they wanted something to eat."

"Possibly. Or maybe to feed someone else, eh? Maybe a chef looking to feed discerning clientele. When someone has a real need for something, they will pay for it. But without a need, even the finest piece of beef is merely a piece of dead bull is it not?"

"Well, of course, people buy the things they buy to achieve something. Otherwise there would be no need for the purchase. That's just common sense."

"Is it? Then why do so many salespeople talk to customers about the product and not the result, hmm?"

"To teach them about it."

"Really?"

"Absolutely. Customers require an education, a presentation. They need to see how things are. What they do."

"So would that be classed as selling *at* someone or helping them to achieve their aim?"

"It would be telling them what something is - for their own good."

"For their own good?" Barnabas leant on his stick and laughed, and said, "Fabulous. Yes. We all like to be made to feel inadequate and stupid by strangers do we not?"

"That's not what I meant…"

"Maybe not, but that is what you would do according to what you've just stated. But, customers do not want a lecture from you and they certainly don't want some juvenile in a bad suit forcing his wares upon them, while being told it's for their own good. No, they want their problem solved with as little expense, as quickly and painlessly as possible, by someone who knows what they're doing."

"So if you're saying that I can't tell them what they need, what would you suggest?"

"You find out what they're trying to achieve and deliver the solution."

"That's what I said."

"No. No. No. It's not! You want to tell me all about the things you have to sell. That is not the same at all. Humor me. If you buy a spade, what do you actually want?"

"A hole."

"Absolutely! So we ask about the hole, it's intended depth, the ground to be dug, about the man who will be doing the digging."

"But he just wants a spade. He knows all about his own hole."

"But *we* don't, do we? How do you advise a man on a situation you don't understand?"

"Badly?"

"Ha! Badly, yes, exactly. There are hundreds of choices for our digger. Dainty spades for turning over pretty herbaceous borders, spades that'll last a lifetime digging roads, spades with handles designed to reduce blistering, shovels, trowels, the list could go on and on. But nobody simply wants a spade. They want the right tool for the job at hand. Let's try another one. A man buys a pen, but he doesn't want a pen he wants to…?"

"Write?"

"Absolutely. He buys a watch, but actually needs?"

"To tell the time? Look professional and smart?"

"Now you're getting it. How about glue?"

"To stick something together."

"Yes! What if he came to purchase a house?"

"Warmth, security, respect."

"Perfect! A book?"

"Entertainment, knowledge, distraction, enlightenment."

"Fabulous. You see what you're doing? You are discovering the conversation that the customer wants to have, instead of the dreadfully limiting presentation you would have given him. And in doing so, you can help him to make a truly wonderful buying decision. Well done, my boy, well done."

Simeon gleamed with pride, as he felt a light shine on him through the dark. Another piece of a puzzle falling into place.

"Why had I not realized this before? It seems so…obvious?"

"Obvious? Possibly. Sometimes, common sense is only obvious once you have been shown it to be so. Only after a shortcut has been revealed is it an obvious time saver. Before that, it had remained completely unknown to everyone but the enlightened. You can't know what you don't know and, therefore, never seek anyone's tutorage of the subject."

"So now that I understand that it's actually the thing they're going to do with it that's important, I just need to change my presentation slightly."

"No. Now you learn about the greatest tool available to any salesman. I'm going to give you an introduction into something that will help customers recognize the value of your offer all by themselves."

And with that, Barnabas picked up his stick and went deeper into the market where the shadows became shorter and voices began to echo and merge into one.

# CHAPTER 7
## The Astonishing Alchemic
## Properties of Appropriate Questions

B ARNABAS POINTED HIS WALKING STICK towards a bench across the cobbled yard. Once they were both settled, he continued.

"This next nugget of salesmanship cannot be perfected in a single afternoon. However, once you have it mastered, your competition will continuously believe you possess some mystical customer attracting formula. The truth of, course, will be far less dramatic. You will simply be asking the appropriate questions."

"Is that all? But everybody does that."

"Do they? I don't think so. Oh no. For some reason salesmen spend most of their time asking questions they already know the answers to. They rarely ask to discover anything new. Their efforts are focused on finding a way to present their product pitch. Tell me. Why would you ask me a question?"

"To receive an answer."

"What if you already knew the answer?"

"I wouldn't ask. That would be a waste of time."

"My time or yours?"

"Both."

"Quite so. Quite right. So, during the process of a sale, what questions would you ask me?"

"I don't know. Lots of different ones. It would depend."

"It would depend? Fair enough. So why would you ask them? To what purpose would you employ all these *different* questions?"

"To sell you something."

"How very noble. Sell me what?"

"Whatever it was I needed to sell you."

"So then, what are your questions for? Why don't you just sell it to me?"

"Because the questions create a conversation. They enable me to build a level of rapport. Without them, it would sound as if I was just going straight for the sale."

"But you are, aren't you? That's exactly what you're doing. Your questions are simply being used to disguise it. Your questions are nothing more than a polite mask."

"In a way, yes."

"So what happened to asking me a question to receive a useful answer?"

"I...I was...what I meant was..."

"Ha, don't tie yourself in knots, my boy. I am well aware that you have never given this much thought before today. Very few people ever do."

Simeon felt he had to redeem himself somehow, explain himself a little better.

"I believe I would ask questions to suit the situation at hand, to ask questions that would allow me to help. But I have no idea how I would describe them to you. So come on, then. What *type* of questions do *you* think I should be asking?"

"Well, initially, I would like you to work on understanding that there are only two types of questions."

"Only two?"

"Yes. Those which open up a conversation and those which close it down."

"To what end?"

"I will get to that shortly, bear with me. First of all, let me tell you about the first type, those that are used to open up a conversation. They really are quite easy to get to grips with. You see they all start with one of six words - who, what, why, where, when, and how."

"Who, what, why, where, when, and how. And what is so wonderful about those?"

"What is so wonderful? Excellent open question, my boy. You see these six words are impossible to say yes or no to. That's what. When you put these words at the beginning of a question, the answer must convey some level of detail."

"How so?"

"There you go again, without even recognizing that you are doing it."

"What?"

"And again. Using open questions, my boy. You are using open questions."

"This is nonsense. It's just good use of English. There isn't another way of asking questions."

"So you might think. However, if you were to use closed questions, I would be able to answer in a simple yes or no – and you would free me from the need to explain myself."

"And so what of these closed questions. How do they begin?"

"That's even easier, my boy. Every other question, which does not start with those six words, is a closed question."

"How so?"

"Do you like apples?"

"I beg your pardon?"

"Do - you - like - apples?"

"Yes."

"There you go. Closed question. Yes or no answer."

"Oh, and is that important?"

"Absolutely! That's how most of the population communicate, grunting at each other, thinking they're holding in-depth conversations. Not successful people though. They know that closed questions cannot expand their understanding of a subject. However, they are aware that they have a great number of other uses."

"Such as?"

"Commitment for one. Will you be joining me for dinner tonight?"

"Yes. Thank you."

"There you go. Closed question leading to commitment."

"Very clever, I'm sure."

"I assure you, I'm not trying to be clever, just trying to explain in as practical way as possible. But there are other uses too. Confirmation of facts is another. How old are you?"

"Twenty one."

"Twenty one?"

"Yes…oh, very good. I see how you did that."

"Ha, I didn't do anything, my boy. Just got some details with an open question and then confirmed them with a closed one that is all."

"And how should I use open questions then?"

"As I said, to garner information. You need to fashion open questions so that you can fully understand facts, put things into context. When you get back this evening try to think of questions so wide and deep that a prospect has no choice but to tell you everything you need to know. Everything they've been waiting desperately to share with someone who can truly help. Funnily enough, the shorter the open question, the bigger the response."

"Do you have an example?"

"Well, you must think of your own, but as an example how about this one. What differences would you like to see? Or, what is it you really want to change?"

"They could end up talking for ages."

"That's the idea. This consultation is about what they need to buy, not what we have to sell."

"And why is that not the same thing?"

"It might be, it might not. That's what the questions are designed to find out."

"So open questions to understand. Closed questions to confirm and gain commitment."

"Spot on! Well done. Right. Let's move on to slightly more complicated ground shall we?"

"If you think I'm ready."

"Oh, I'm sure you'll keep up. What if I could show you how to ask questions that help your prospects recognize the value of working with you?"

"And how would they recognize that if they're doing all the talking?"

"Quite so. Quite right. You're asking, they're answering. But what if their answers uncovered the effects of not receiving the perfect solution, not working with you?"

"That sounds negative."

"It is a little, but without a realisation that a problem might exist, there can be no recognition for the value of the solution."

"I'm sorry, Uncle. This is going straight over my head."

"My sincere apologies, you're right. I'm getting ahead of myself, an example is required. Tell me. What kind of house would you like to live in?"

"Well, I suppose one that would be comfortable enough for a family, and yet recognisable as the home of a gentleman, who has done rather well for himself."

"Very good. What else?"

"I don't know. Gardens. I'd like gardens."

"How big?"

Simeon thought for a moment.

"Big enough for children to have adventures in, long enough for them to run to the end and back and be out of breath on their return."

"Fabulous. And what would happen if there wasn't a garden?"

"Then that wouldn't be acceptable. It just isn't what I have in mind. It's a bit of a dream of mine to have gardens."

"So the garden is important?"

"Absolutely, completely."

"And there you have it."

Simeon's shoulders jolted slightly, his face showing an expression that indicated he thought he'd missed something.

"What? I have what?"

"I asked open questions to understand what you were looking for. Once I uncovered a need, your garden, I asked an effect question regarding the absence of it to make sure it mattered, and then a solution question to help you clarify its value."

"I still do not see how this is helpful to me as a salesman, or in aiding prospects to recognize why they should choose me over another."

"I am aware that it can be easily missed, but once you have the ability to uncover and clarify real needs – the things that really matter – you can discuss in detail how you meet each and every one. Don't you think you would then be viewed as a preferable supplier versus the competition?"

"But that wouldn't change my sales pitch, though, would it? I would still end up going through the same presentation?"

"No. You'd be focusing your conversation on the bits that mattered."

"But what if the competition has something that could do the job just as well?"

"It's suitability and value would probably be lost in their vast meaningless, and mostly pointless, presentation."

"Because they tried to show everything rather than the bits the customer saw value in?"

Barnabas smiled broadly.

"Precisely. You know I think you've got it, my boy. That's what marks out the successful from the nearly-rans. Focusing on what makes people itch rather than continuously presenting an entire catalogue of scratches."

"But that's not selling is it? It's more consultative, the kind of conversation a doctor would have or a lawyer."

"And why shouldn't you be viewed in such a way?"

"Because all I do is sell things."

"No, my boy. We've been through this." Barnabas pounded the end of his stick into the cobbles to emphasize each word. "You –

help – people. You are an expert in your field, who genuinely helps other human beings. Take pride in that, stop hawking your wares, and get a bit of respect for your profession, and earn some from your prospects. They cannot do this properly without you. Yes, they may have some degree of choice with your competition, but there will be nobody like you. Nobody else will have their best interests at heart and the perfect solution to their problem."

"Is that how you view being a salesman? Helping people? Delivering perfect solutions?"

"No. It's not how I view being a salesman. It's how I *live* being a salesman."

Simeon smiled at his uncle. He truly respected this man. There was a foundation to his every thought and emotion.

"This," thought Simeon, "is exactly how I wish to become."

"Right." Barnabas jolted Simeon back to reality, picking himself up, and making his way towards the back wall of the market.

"Come on, lad. Things to see, letters to discover."

"Letters? For the word?"

"Quite so. Quite right. Now then, how's your Greek history, hmm?"

"Not bad, I suppose. I'm certainly not an expert."

"Neither am I." Barnabas beamed back at the young man hurrying to catch up. "What does the word *agora* mean to you?"

"Ah, I know this. It was the central market place where people came to do business and discuss matters of political importance."

"Exactly, spot on! So when the architect of this fabulous market created his original designs, the *agora* is precisely what he had in mind. Which is why, if you look at the vast wall in front of you, you should see your next clue."

"It's just a big brick wall."

"Ah, those wonderful powers of observation kicking in again I see. Stop looking at individual bricks and step back, view the entire wall."

Simeon stepped back and stared hard. Some bricks were brown, some were red. It really was just a big brick wall.

"Hold on. What's that?" Simeon thought he might have seen a slight pattern. "The red bricks form a line from the floor at the right corner to the middle of the roof and then back down to the opposite corner."

"Do they?" Barnabas chuckled.

"Yes. Look." Simeon turned to his uncle, pointing at the wall. "And then there is a line across the middle. It's an *A*, a capital *A*."

"Well done, my boy. An *A* for *agora*, eh?"

"Ha, yes. *A* for *agora*. So I now have an *N* and an *A*."

"Indeed. Right. Make a note. We must return back to the Club so that I can run through some exercises to help you get to grip with those tricky questioning techniques, eh?"

And with that Barnabas headed straight out towards the front of the market, with Simeon trying to follow directly behind, while still attempting to write the new letter in his journal.

*Journal Entry*
*Monday, 5th September 1887*

I'm quite embarrassed to write this, but I need to get a bit of respect for myself and my profession.

On top of that, I cannot believe how long I have been ignoring what my prospects were actually asking me for.

All this time, I have been selling what I had, rather than recognizing what it was they needed.

They don't want to hear about my product, my service, my means to make a living.

They want someone to show them how their lives can be enriched or made easier. They want solutions to their problems. They want honest, understandable advice.

Two things were shown to me today, which as I now write, seem so ridiculously obvious, and yet I have been blissfully unaware of each of them for my entire life.

First, I'll record what I've learnt on the subject of what I sell.

What it actually is means little to anyone other than me, but what it does and how it helps, means everything to those who require it.

I must turn myself around so that I am viewing life as my prospects see it. Only then can I start addressing their issues, help to prevent their pain, and advise on solutions to their problems.

Second, I will stop simply pitching at people, talking incessantly for fear that they might ask me to leave before I've got everything out.

Trying to tell them what is good for them, without knowing a thing about their situation or circumstance.

From now on my prospects input will be the major element of all conversations.

I will ask questions that are so wide and open they will feel the need to speak for a week.

Then from the information that they give to me, I will mold solutions designed specifically for them.

I will embrace these fundamentals, for they are the foundation on which I will build my success.

# CHAPTER 8
## The Third Rule: Plot Your Course

THE TWO MEN APPROACHED the church in respectful silence, joining the short line of mourners, who shuffled slowly through the elaborately decorated arch of grinning skulls, and then up the short path into the church.

Following the service, they strolled across to the center of the graveyard. The silence broken intermittently by crows watching from the thin, finger-like branches overhead, and the muffled clattering of hooves from the busy street on the other side of the building.

Barnabas spoke first.

"I wonder what he had planned to do today."

"What who had planned?"

"That poor chap whose funeral we just attended. I wonder what he wanted to be doing right at this moment?"

"Breathing would probably have been high on the list."

"Yes. Quite so. Quite right. Breathing. Quite so. And what did you think the other members of the funeral party thought of him, eh?"

"Well, they spoke very highly of him as I recall. Loving husband and father, loyal friend and employee. Taken in his prime with prosperous years ahead of him."

"Not anymore he hasn't, hey? Not anymore! And tell me, young man, what do you wish your obituary to say about you? Hmmm? What do you want people to say about you when you are gone?"

"Oh, I don't know. I always tried my best, I suppose."

"Good God, boy, is that it?" Barnabas turned as if addressing a congregation. "Thank you all for coming today, as we say goodbye to a fine young man, taken in his prime. Would anybody like to add anything? Why yes. I'd like to say he always tried his best. Thank you for that. Right. Cover him with dirt, try not to leave anything poking out. Just do your best to bury him."

"That is a little unfair. It isn't for me to decide what people say about me at my own funeral."

Barnabas spun on his heels to face the young man and pointed his stick at Simeon's chest.

"But it is, my boy. They shouldn't be discussing the life of anyone else at your funeral. And tell me, who else but you has the power to choose how your life is to be lived? May I pose you a conundrum?"

"If you wish."

"Good. Let's imagine you were on a train to Edinburgh, traveling to attend a meeting of the most vital importance. On no account could it be missed or arrived at late, but after traveling for over an hour, the ticket inspector informs you that you are actually on a train to Bristol. The completely wrong train. Traveling in completely the wrong direction! Would you just continue onwards to see what the weather was like in Bristol? Decide to send word to your meeting in Edinburgh that unfortunately you would not be able to attend?"

"No, of course not. I would find a way to get off the train, find a new route to Edinburgh. I would find a way to make that meeting."

"I'm sure you would." Barnabas smiled. "In fact, I have no doubt that you would go through hell or high water to attend. We've already recognized that the appointment was set in stone, it was of vital importance. You had to get there."

"So what has this got to do with my funeral?"

"A great deal, my boy, a very great deal. Most people recognize the importance of diary dates and so make short-term projects look like fairly easy tasks. And yet, why is it that they live their lives in a completely different fashion?"

"I didn't know they did."

"Oh yes. The vast majority of the populace would never think of setting themselves any deadlines for the achievement of their dreams. They may have a vague notion they will get older and that one day they will probably die, but it all seems a long way away, and tomorrow will bring its own share of problems and pressing issues to fill their time."

Simeon wrapped his coat around his chest and sat on a large, stone tomb.

"But that is what I was saying before. Surely doing ones best is quite admirable isn't it?"

"Is it? Could trying your hardest, but never being quite good enough ever be acceptable to anyone? Is that what your dreams are made of?"

"No. I've told you. I want to do my best, excel."

"And yet you don't know what that looks like, do you? So it's all a bit vague isn't it?"

Simeon had to agree that his future plans, although quite grand, were like pictures painted in fog. Nothing he could put his finger on. No dream ever remained unchanged long enough to take on any weight or substance, just a notion of something better waiting for him somewhere in the future. He turned to his uncle looking a little lost.

"I must admit, I was hoping that it would all somehow just fall into place."

"But you know deep down that the world really doesn't work that way, don't you? Tell me. Do you have the title of Rule Number Three?"

Simeon once again took out his letter and scanned through the script.

"Rule Number Three is *plot your course.*"

"Plot your course it is indeed. And fabulously well-named it is too. Simple piece of thinking this, but so easily overlooked. You always have to know where you are trying to get to if you ever want to arrive."

"Simple?" Simeon scoffed at what appeared to be a pointless statement. "Simple and obvious!"

"Simple and obvious?" Barnabas chuckled to himself. "You'd think so, wouldn't you? It certainly sounds it, but on a day-to-day basis, we are all so busy, so lost in the whirlwind that our lives become, that that simple message just gets lost. We forget that we need to set our minds on an actual date and destination and then work towards getting there. Just like in our train story."

"But it's clear that all the effort in the world would be wasted without deciding where you're actually going."

"Quite so. Quite right. Let's take a look at another similar scenario, shall we? Let's say you were sailing a boat and were blown off course. Would you correct yourself when the weather allowed, get yourself back on track?"

"Of course. It would be foolish and perilous not to."

"Of course it would, and yet because most people haven't set themselves any course with regards to their life. They have no idea whether or not they are being blown in any useful direction whatsoever. They are just at the whim of wherever the winds of life take them. And what happens then?"

"They're going to end up wherever the breeze takes them."

"Indeed, and worse than that. With no plan of their own, they end up being part of somebody else's plan and, my dear boy, if all you are is a line in somebody else's journal, then you have most definitely relinquished control of your own destiny. You are satisfying someone else's happiness, helping someone else create their dreams and fortune rather than creating your own."

Simeon knew instinctively that this was good advice. He was only too aware of how he hoped and dreamed of wealth and greatness but had made no real plans to achieve either.

"So what do you suggest. How do I begin to plot my course?"

"Well, as with all things, you must get it down on paper. Get the link working between the mechanical and the cerebral, ingrain your thoughts and dreams deep into your subconscious, because that is where it will start to work for you. Filing away all the unimportant nonsense that filled your day, and organising the in-tray of important business, and even though you are not aware of the fact, your subconscious will be working you towards your goal."

"So, I simply write down how wealthy I wish to become and just let my brain do all the work without further effort?"

"Don't be so ridiculous." Barnabas looked extremely indignant. "Dreaming and becoming are completely separate parts of the process. However, they are both as important as each other. Never discount how powerful your dreams are. If you cannot visualize what it is you wish to become, then the brain doesn't have the first clue how to get you there."

"So how do I go about cataloging my dreams?"

"Very well phrased, dear boy, nicely put. When you return this evening you are going to write down your goals and aspirations."

"You want me to write out what I want in the future?"

"Absolutely, but I don't want you to try and work out where you want to get to. I want you to start right at the end and then work backwards!"

"I beg your pardon?"

"We have already discussed that moving continuously forward doesn't necessarily get us to where we want to be, just somewhere other than where we started. If we want to get to our chosen destination, we must decide where it is and then plot our course to there from where we are now."

"Oh," Simeon said excitedly. "Oh, I see. This is starting to make sense. I was wondering what boats and trains and funerals had to do with anything."

"Simply metaphors, my boy, but the funeral is probably the most important. When you return this evening make sure that no one will disturb you for a couple of hours, clear your mind, prepare your desk and journal, sit down and close your eyes. I want you to imagine that today's funeral had been your own. That the congregation had been full of your friends, your family, and your colleagues. You must imagine that it is many, many years from now and that you have lived a life that you were extremely proud of and gloriously happy with."

Simeon was fascinated, if not a little unnerved by the morbidity of the scenario. Barnabas stared deep into the eyes of the young man and continued.

"One by one a representative from each part of your life will walk slowly to the pulpit and read their speech. There will be a family member representing your entire family, all of them past, present, and future, grandparents, parents, children, and grandchildren. Then a representative of your friends and acquaintances will step forward. After that, your colleagues will be represented, as will all of your future customers. Write down everything, as they deliver their eulogies. These people are putting into words the perfect life that you currently dream of living."

"I find the process of writing down how wonderful I am, or might be, rather bizarre and immodest."

"Ha, modesty be damned! That is the whole point of this process. If you have designed your last day on earth, if you have decided how you wish to be thought of on your deathbed, only then can you start to plot a course to that point, to your ideal final destination. Then, whenever you feel that you are being blown off course, you can correct yourself. If you feel that you are suddenly on the wrong train, you simply make the appropriate plans to get back on the right one. Without these self-set guidelines and directions, you are at the whim of wherever life takes you, whether you think you are in charge or not."

"So, as useful as this sounds, and I concede it does, how will it help me to become an extremely successful salesman?"

"Good question. I'm glad you asked. First of all, it gives you an opportunity to work out what is important to you, where your values lie, the very foundation upon which all your decisions should be made. Once you have finished the funeral exercise, read through the words and find statement groups that have some common thread. It is vitally important that you write these down as targets in sentence form, detailed as the things you want to become."

"Like what?"

"Well, if during their speeches your customers said they admired your honesty and your friends commented upon your loyalty, you would write sentences such as, 'I want to be remembered as always being honest,' or 'I want people to say that I never let them down.' Things like that."

"Oh, I see. And how many should I write?"

"As many as required."

"Remind me again why we're doing this."

"Because it's your own personal statement of who you want to become, based on how you wish to be remembered. You know, I have never met a young man who recognizes the true value in this exercise, and yet I have met hundreds of old men who wished someone had shared it with them in their youth. Humor me and finish it this evening."

"I will."

"Good. Now, once you have your death sorted out you can get started on your life."

"I should think so," mumbled Simeon.

"What was that?"

"Nothing, Uncle. Do please carry on."

Barnabas raised an eyebrow and continued.

"Yes. Indeed. Next, you should write upon a new sheet of paper the following four headings:

- My age in one years' time
- My age in five years' time

- My age in ten years' time
- My age in twenty years' time

Below each heading, write the position in business you wish to hold and the annual salary you expect to receive."

"And what else?"

"Nothing. Your age gives the goal a deadline. And the annual salary gives it an amount, while the inclusion of a desired position will point to the things you must learn and achieve, in order to become that which you wish to become."

"But I've already thought this through previously. Everything I can confidently envisage becoming doesn't get me even slightly close to my target position and desired wealth."

"That is because you can only see your current horizon. Every time you move nearer to your desired destination, new horizons will become clear. New, previously hidden, opportunities will come into view. With that in mind, it is important to make sure that each new target is very slightly out of your comfort zone. Writing the figures should make you feel just a little uneasy, make you question your own ambition."

"Even if it's beyond me? Unachievable?"

"It will always be achievable. Don't you worry about that. Everything you could wish to become has already been achieved by someone before you. Anyway, no one ever reached the top of a mountain by digging underneath it." Barnabas smiled and tapped the handle of his stick onto Simeon's stomach. "You must always listen to your gut."

"But what if I wish to become more than I am, to achieve that which is really beyond me?"

"You mean currently beyond you, don't you? What happened to adopting the positive? You have your whole life to become what you wish to become. As long as we know where we are going, we can prepare ourselves for the journey. That which is currently beyond your capabilities now, does not have to be so forever. You just have to work the *becoming something* into the time frame of the plan."

"But what if I can't wait? What if I wish to miss all this and just *become* successful?"

"Can a farmer plants his seeds and then demand the crops to grow before harvest? Eh, can he?"

Simeon raised his eyebrows in acquiescent realisation and smiled reluctantly.

"No. Of course not, Uncle. He would have to wait for his crops to grow into edible produce."

"Quite so. Quite right. There is a natural way of things. If you put in the effort and focus towards a goal, you will get there quicker than most. However, you cannot become something new without putting in the appropriate effort, can you? Just as a seed cannot grow into an ear of corn without the appropriate time, sunlight, water, and care. That is just the way of things."

"That doesn't appease my impatience though."

Barnabas nodded an understanding nod.

"I know. I know. We are all impatient you know. Even men of my years, but let me give you a line that has helped me to put things into perspective. *Men constantly miscalculate what they can do in a day, and grossly underestimate what can be achieved in a year."*

Once again, Simeon smiled. Though still frustrated with a lack of any quick fix, something to jettison him to immediate riches, he understood everything his uncle had shared and was excited with regards to returning once again to his journal to plan out his future success.

"Uncle, you mentioned that one of the criteria was being exact. How specific do I have to be?"

"On paper, as vague or detailed as you feel inclined. However in your mind, you must be able to visualize every last part of your dream, smell every scent and taste every flavour. Dream it continuously." Barnabas tapped Simeon's forehead and heart with his middle finger. "If it is not real - here and here - then it will never take shape out here, in the real world."

"Well, that's all very well for the big, life-changing stuff, but not really very useful for the day-to-day salesman's work is it."

"Quite the contrary."

"Really? How can such a vast, end-of-days, plan-your-life idea like this work, or be useful in individual sales situations?"

"Actually in exactly the same way. One of the biggest problems with your average sales call is that the salesman doesn't know what he is trying to achieve. He hasn't worked out the end of the journey. So he sets off and just hopes he walks out with …something."

"Surely not. People don't hold meetings without a set outcome in mind."

"Of course they do, and be honest with yourself. So do you. And what you're all missing is that a sales call is like any other journey. It needs planning. Start with your chosen destination and then work backwards to see how it is easiest achieved."

Then, with a sudden sweeping motion, Barnabas pointed his stick back to the large wooden doors.

"Come with me. I want to share something else with you before we leave."

Before Simeon could ask anything more, Barnabas had marched back inside the now empty church.

Simeon followed directly, his vision taking a moment to readjust. He found Barnabas sitting next to a memorial stone set into the west wall, beckoning him to come over.

"This, my boy," Barnabas's booming voice echoed around the church, "is the final resting place of Edward Varda. The founding father of our wonderful Club."

As Simeon approached he saw a large, rectangular stone, pale and smooth, with nothing but a raised *V* carved across its face.

"Where are the dates and details, the final messages from family and friends?"

"On the inside."

"How utterly pointless. Who's going to see them in there?"

"All those, who were here on the day, saw them. Some of us even wrote them."

"I'm sorry. I didn't mean to be insensitive."

"You weren't. Don't worry. Actually, it's what he wanted people to say. Just his sense of humor. You see, he plotted his course to perfection. What was said was only relevant to those present and every word spoken was exactly what he had worked towards all his life. He just wanted this symbol on the outside so that anyone, who wanted to visit, knew where he was, but that man left a legacy and an institution that says so much more about him than any single stone ever could."

"That's something to aspire to then."

"It most certainly is. I reckon when your tombstone makes up part of an intricate puzzle designed for a secret club's induction process, you've pretty much etched yourself into the history books."

"The *V*? The next letter?"

Barnabas smiled a mischievous smile.

"Of course it is. Otherwise it really would be a pointless piece of stone wouldn't it?"

With that he lifted himself on to his stick and headed out of the church and back towards the large, foreboding gates.

Outside the funeral party was gathering to make the short journey aboard the necropolis train to Brookwood Cemetery.

Simeon and Barnabas stood and watched the group leave mournfully, taking the deceased to his final resting place.

"Who was he then?" asked Simeon

"Who was who?"

"That poor deceased gentleman, of course"

"Oh, him! I have absolutely no idea!"

And with that Barnabas hailed a cab and left Simeon alone,

walking towards the nearby bridge, mulling over the day's events, and wondering how to plot the course of the rest of his life.

## Journal Entry
### Tuesday, 6th September 1887

Unwittingly, I have sailed through my entire life, so far, with neither direction nor destination.

I had a vague instinct to reach dry land every once in a while for supplies, but never anything more than that.

The reward for living my life in this manner? An existence like that of a seagull picking up scraps from the back of a fishing boat. Surviving day to day. Nothing left for tomorrow and no idea what tomorrow should be.

To my shame, I had never thought to ask anything of the future, and yet woke each and every day embittered because it was never what I needed it to be.

The big plan? The things I desired? The end result? I had no idea what any of those things were, and because of that, I never took the time to work out what I needed to do in order to posses them.

Respect, wealth, property, friendship, even love. Did I expect to simply fall over each of them as I strolled aimlessly through the years? Was I expecting my whole life to be some form of lucky accident?

Although I had tried hard not to show it today, the sudden realisation made me feel more lost than I have ever felt before.

Until this afternoon, I have been wandering around, fumbling my way through days and months and years. How naive. How arrogant.

But now, this very evening, I have imagined a future worth living. I have visualized the coming years and I am excited beyond belief.

I know now what I require to be happy in terms of money and position and the personal matters of the soul, of the heart and the mind.

I see what I have to become and I recognize the time it will take.

I have plotted my course back from where I eventually wish to arrive. My future is designed and lies here before me, on a single piece of paper.

# CHAPTER 9
## The Fourth Rule: Take the Journey

THE NEXT MORNING THEY met at eight and began the short journey to the docks.

As they stepped from the cab, Simeon caught his first sight of the enormous sailing vessels bustling with activity. A variety of men, many of whom Simeon quickly decided he would not wish to meet after dark, hauled sacks and casks onto the ship's decks or threw them down to roll precariously across the quay.

Barnabas stopped and called up to a particularly gnarly-faced individual, busily directing the frenzied activity aboard a vast clipper.

"Where are you headed, my good man?"

"Trade visit to the Americas."

"Fabulous! Marvelous! God's speed!"

The old salt gave a casual salute together with a slightly bemused look and got back to his work. Barnabas and Simeon continued up to the railings overlooking the end of the harbor and watched the gulls dip and dive across the top of the water. Some were fighting over discarded scraps of food, others soaring to the top of the sails and floating on the breeze.

Barnabas took a deep breath, filled his lungs, and smiled.

"This is a fabulous spot, don't you think? There is always a huge sense of adventure and anticipation around such places. Great and wondrous escapades awaiting brave young men, who embark on the journeys others would fear to begin, eh?"

Simeon nodded as he looked on in awe. This was shipping and industry on a scale he had never witnessed before.

"It's just all so…impressive!"

"Indeed it is, although we aren't here to contemplate the majesty of the mighty British trade routes or those who would traverse their corridors. We are here to visualize Rule Number Four…*take the journey.*"

"I think I would have probably grasped the concept of taking a journey without coming all the way out here."

"Maybe. Maybe not. However, we would never have seen this if we'd gone anywhere else."

As he spoke, Barnabas banged his stick firmly on the ground. Simeon looked to the floor and realized they were standing in the middle of an enormous mariner's star. Part fresco, part mosaic, it lay beneath them, decoratively surrounded by an assortment of clouds, cherubs, and mermaids. At the center, a large compass exhibited only two letters: a capital *E* correctly indicating east and, rather oddly, the letter *I* stood opposite in place of a *W*, pointing behind them to the west.

Simeon's eyes lit up.

"These are the next two letters, aren't they?"

"No. You can only have one."

"But there are two. Which one is it?"

"Ha! That is something that you must work out, while we have our little chat."

"Do we really need to? This rule doesn't need much of an explanation. I understand the thinking. Now that I have plotted my course, I must take the journey. So you can just tell me which one of these letters I need, and we can move straight on to Rule Number Five."

"Can we indeed?" Barnabas chuckled to himself. "Well, you're partly right. The journey referred to in Rule Number Four is indeed a natural continuation of last night's exercise, which by the sounds of it, you thoroughly enjoyed."

"Yes. I found it surprisingly easy once begun."

"Good for you! And by making that plan you have differentiated yourself from more than ninety percent of the population. You are one of the few, who has a clear direction, a decisive plan of action. But I'm afraid that field is cut down in similar numbers once again by today's rule."

"And why would that be?"

"Excellent question. It's because most people, who create life changing plans, will never see them through to the end."

"Why would anyone go to all that trouble to achieve nothing?"

"Oh come, my boy. You know as many people as I do, who set themselves resolutions on New Year's Eve only to fall short before Burns Night. Plans are easy to make, dreams are easy to dream. But putting your back into it? A little bit of hard graft and discipline? That is just too scary and far too much effort for the masses."

"But I'm ready to get going. I have set my mind on starting as soon as I return home."

"I'm sure you have, my boy. I'm sure you have. These sailors have their charts too. However, they know that the secret of getting somewhere is to set sail, to leave port."

"I assure you. I fully understand and grasp the concept. I am with you. Nothing happens if you're not heading in the right direction."

"Quite so. Quite right. It doesn't. But no. This rule isn't about the direction. It's about making it happen, doing something with it. The challenge for you today is to take the first item of your plan and do it this afternoon."

"But I've told you. I'm going to start once I arrive home."

"Why wait?"

"Because I can't do it here. I'm not ready, I haven't yet…"

"Ready? No one is ever ready, my boy. But some do what they plan to do and some never will. The difference between the two is that the first group understand that they need to start somewhere, so they do so. Straight away."

"No, really. I'm really not ready!"

"Ha! You can't plough a field by turning it over in your mind. Either you get out there and plough it or it doesn't get done. Tell me. What's really stopping you from starting today?"

"I don't know…it's just not right. And anyway, I didn't say I wouldn't start. Just that I wouldn't start right away."

"Fair enough. So you're afraid then?"

"No. Why would I be afraid?"

"Why? Because your plan is the edge of a cliff. It's another step outside your comfort zone and every move you make in that direction has the potential for failure, disgrace, and humiliation."

"Steady on."

"Well, tell me I'm wrong."

"Well, I…I don't think you're right."

"I'll take that as a positive. Tell me. Have you ever thought how terrifying setting sail on one of these things must be?" Barnabas stretched out his arm back towards the clipper. "Lives and cargo are at risk. Not to mention personal fortunes and investments."

"So why would anyone go?"

"I don't know." Barnabas smiled. "Seems ridiculous, doesn't it?"

Simeon gestured to the nearest ship.

"And I see some of these young men don't look old enough to leave their mother's side. Never mind sail across the ocean."

"Maybe everyone on board feels they're as ready as they need to be."

"Or maybe they have fooled themselves of such."

"Is there a difference?"

Simeon couldn't believe what he was hearing.

"Of course there is! You are ready or you are not, believing otherwise is folly."

"What if you are definitely ready and still don't go. What is that called?"

"Choice - free will - deciding not to do so."

"Possibly. Although I put it to you that it could also be described as fear, a waste of talent, an opportunity turned to nothing, an adventure ignored, an..."

Simeon, clearly irritated and not wishing to listen, began to speak over his uncle.

"Whatever! You can call it one thing. I can call it another. I don't see how I'm learning anything new here. Is there really anything more to say on the subject?"

Barnabas realized he had struck a nerve and smiled again.

"More? Quite a lot actually. I want to share with you why this rule is so vitally important to every sales call you will ever make, every obstacle you will ever face, and every point in every plan that you will lay precisely down on every page of every journal you will ever own."

"At last, a connection to sales. So how does this impact on one of my sales calls then?"

"You really have become quite grumpy, Nephew. Do take a breath of air." Barnabas tapped his stick on the railing and raised an eyebrow. "You're not going to get the best out of me, dear boy, if I don't see the best in you."

Simeon felt a shot of embarrassment fire through him. He had started the day feeling so in charge of his destiny. This gentle push designed to ease him out of his comfort zone, to make him do something quicker than he felt at ease with, had wrangled him, although he wasn't entirely sure why. He suddenly recognized how this mood was impacting upon the conversation, and taking a deep breath, he turned back to Barnabas rather sheepishly.

"My apologies, Uncle. I am, of course, interested and keen to continue."

"I know you are. Believe me, I know exactly how you feel right now." Barnabas tapped his stick back onto the mariner's star. "This E stands for everything that is external, out there, away from you. While the I stands for everything that is internal, personal, to do with you. The question is which one will have the greatest impact on your success while you take the journey?"

"I'm not following you."

"I don't expect you to straight away, but bear with me. Let's look at the ship analogy again, shall we? Let's say you are the captain. You have your map, your ship, your crew, and you are ready to set sail. So you do. Two weeks out, you hit a terrible storm. What can you change about the storm?"

"Nothing. It is the weather."

"Quite so. Quite right. So how do you all survive?"

"With experienced hands, people who are ready to deal with any eventuality, instinct."

"So, is it ever the right time to be in a storm?"

"It has nothing to do with the time being right or wrong. Storms just happen."

"Indeed. Storms just happen. And so it is with business. The only time you have is the where and when of right now. There will always be good times, bad times, hard times, and complete disasters. However, there is no other option but to be where you are, when you are. That is a universal truth for everyone. The important thing is how you respond, what you decide to do, and when you decide to do it."

"That's not very comforting."

"It's not meant to be. It just is. So when you find yourself in a storm, what's going to save you? The things you can control or the things that you cannot?"

"The things I can control."

"Exactly! And what kind of things are those?"

"My actions? Possibly the actions of those who might listen to my instruction?"

"Spot on, dear boy, spot on! You may not be aware, but during every deep rut in the history of business there have been men, who have become extremely successful while the majority failed. Sometime in the future, when business slumps and there appears to be no solution in sight, you will hear others moaning about and blaming the things that are completely out of their control, wasting hour after hour on elements, which cannot be changed. Meanwhile, you, my boy, you will be focusing your efforts on the only thing that matters. The response which ensures you reach your destination."

Simeon looked skeptical.

"I recognize why that may have been good advice a while ago, in simpler times, but there are many challenges in today's markets. There are many elements much more complex than when you were a younger man."

"Do you think so?" Barnabas grinned. "Maybe you're right. Tell me, then. If that is the case, who will be best equipped to navigate these new unchartered waters of the future? The man who believes he can master the uncontrollable?"

"Well, clearly, no. Anyone, who cocoons himself from the truth, is sure to fail."

"Indeed. Like King Canute, eh? Sitting at the water's edge, demanding the tide go back because he told it to?"

"Yes, exactly. Just foolish."

"Good! Right. Just for fun, let's make you a captain. What if you needed to set sail from here today? When would you leave? How would you ensure you reached your destination?"

"Well, I would be working to a deadline, so would have to leave as soon as it was safe to do so. I suppose after that you're up against the elements. I'd have to be prepared for whatever happened or we'd all perish."

"And the things you weren't ready for?"

"I would have to pick it up on the spot."

"Absolutely. You'd just have to learn on the job. And how would moaning or procrastinating help in those situations?"

"They wouldn't. They'd more than likely get us all killed."

"Quite so. Quite right. And how about if you started your plan today, instead of next week. Would that get anybody killed?"

"No. Of course it wouldn't. Don't be so ridiculous."

"I'm not. We've just established that starting today would harm no one. Surely adding an unnecessary week onto the length of this life-changing plan is the ridiculous part."

"Possibly. Although an extra week wouldn't kill anyone either."

"No, you're right. The only thing that suffers here is your success. Listen, there's no need for us to disagree. You're right. All I'm asking is that you ensure some guaranteed movement."

"And how would you suggest I achieve that."

"Well, you know where you are trying to get to. Do you not?"

"Let's say that I do."

"Then the direction is not in question, just the distance you are able to travel each day. You see continuous movement is the important thing here. Those who remain in one position and then lie to themselves about their progress are the ones in real trouble."

"So getting gradually closer is the trick?"

"Absolutely. Let's imagine a sales situation for a moment. You may have an overall target to achieve with each prospect, but if you are going to have an ideal outcome for each call, should you not also have a tolerable outcome to fall back on? Something you are willing to put up with if things don't go completely to plan, but something that still moves things forward ever so slightly?"

"How would that help?"

"The same way that a captain doesn't always wait for the perfect wind to catch his sails. He works with what he has to hand and moves as far and fast as possible. Currently, you are approaching each opportunity with a single possible outcome and when that doesn't happen you fool yourself that there was nothing more that you could have done. The future is a fabulous place to bury your success, Simeon.

Don't allow your imagination to color events as lesser men would, and see movement in motionless things. Be brave with your actions. All these ships are currently safe at anchor but that is not what they were designed for is it? Your job is not to remain anchored and safe. Your job is to move closer to your destination at every attempt. You can deliver change and solutions to those who desperately need them, but to do so you must take them somewhere new, and that will take courage."

Simeon looked back down at the compass below them.

"So you think I should concentrate on becoming fit for the journey, rather than worrying about the journey itself, and making sure I don't waste any time."

"Well, you should try not to worry about the journey at all, although that's easier said than done. You need to view it as simply the space in-between you and your destination. If you can be better than the complications it puts in your way, you will reach the end square, start to worry about it, or fall short of its obstacles and you don't arrive."

"And if I'm not up to it?"

Barnabas put his hand on his nephew's shoulder and tapped his stick on the floor.

"When things get tough, remember this mariner's star. Bring to mind that everything external is designed as a challenge. A test sent to ensure you are actually worthy of acquiring your goal and reward. Recognize them as such and you will always find a way to go through, go round, or ignore them as required"

"So the answer is *I*, internal?"

"It is."

"Ha! So I now have *N*, *A* , *V*, and *I*. That's interesting…"

"What is?"

"*NAVI* – it's Latin for ship."

"So it is. So it is."

And with that, Barnabas Kreuz would say nothing further on the subject for the rest of the day.

*Journal Entry*
*Wednesday, 7th September 1887*

What have I been waiting for?

Is it really so much easier to live in dreams and half-concocted plans, while boasting amongst friends of the great deeds that will be achieved in the future, than to actually do something about it?

I now know why I have acted like this. Until you take the first step forward, failure remains reassuringly impossible.

No one can mock your meager achievements or inability to accomplish the simplest of tasks, if they remain figments of your imagination. You can revel, again and again, in the glory of a fairy tale doomed never to appear in reality.

How many times have I raised a glass and said, "Ah, the things we'll do when..." These were empty words, ridiculous bravado.

As soon as I can find the courage to put my plans to action, I will turn from being a "maybe man" into someone whose future success lies completely in his own hands.

There is no point hiding behind any other description. I have been afraid.

Falling has become far more terrifying to me than rising. My dreams were never imprinted upon my subconscious strongly enough to motivate me to take even one step towards them.

But where am I afraid of falling from and to? How can I fall when I'm standing at the bottom rung of a ladder?

So, do I fear climbing to the top and falling from there? Do I fear that I will not belong, not fit in? Do I secretly fear that I'm not good enough for the ladder at all?

Do I believe the ladder is more worthy to reach greater heights than me? Can it be true that the instrument used to climb feels more useful than the climber?

And that brings me to the real decision.

I either begin to move forward now, to become what I want to become, or I do not. If I do not, then I shall not achieve great wealth or the respect I crave. I must give up on those dreams this very night, for I will have made my choice, and that choice was to accept the fear and stay where I am.

Surely that would be a worse fate, having all those who believe that I may yet make something of myself, discover that I never tried or ever had any intention of doing so.

But if I move forward, then surely I can achieve whatever it is that I set my mind upon, even if it has to be by one small step at a time.

If I do fall, will I not simply find myself back here?

If the worst-case scenario is returning to my original start point, wouldn't I simply start again? Redraw the map, plot a new course based on my experiences, recognize that I must reach the destination?

It is the destination that matters.

But I will never get there if I don't start and finish every journey, and these journeys are well worth taking.

# CHAPTER 10
## The Fifth Rule: Design Your Reputation

ARRIVING AT CHANCERY LANE by cab, they entered the tailor's shop through the dull, brown door, accompanied by a shrill tinkle from the bell above their heads, which alerted the owners of new customers.

"Welcome to the Club's official tailors," pronounced Barnabas. "Now, let's get you fitted out with a suit a little more…in line with your new position in society."

"A new suit? I can't afford a new suit and, if you don't mind me asking, what is so disagreeable with my current attire?"

"The suit will be my gift. As for your current attire…well…" Barnabas looked Simeon up and down and then cocked his head to one side. "You may look a little smarter than the gentlemen with whom you currently spend your time. However, you are about to start moving in new circles, new acquaintances, new opportunities."

He took a seat, motioning for the tailor to begin measuring. The short, bald man pulled his glasses across the top of his head down to the bridge of his nose and stretched his tape measure across Simeon's shoulders.

"I do not need you to dress me, Uncle, as grateful as I am for the thought. I find this …unnecessary."

Barnabas flicked through some cloth samples, and then leant onto his stick to raise himself, staring directly into his nephew's eyes.

"This is completely necessary, young man. Have you any concept, any idea at all of how you are portraying yourself? How leaders of industry and commerce would view you at this precise moment?"

Simeon raised a sarcastic eyebrow. "No. I do not. Please, enlighten me."

"If you wish, there's no point tiptoeing round it. You look green, immature. A young boy playing at business, dressing up in the manner in which he believes an actual grown-up would. Your viewpoint of business attire is one of wide-eyed wonder from the nursery door."

Simeon looked suitably aggrieved. Barnabas, however, had already turned back to the cloth samples and continued speaking, oblivious to his nephew's bruised ego.

"A gentleman of ambition is aware of the people he wishes to be associated with both socially and commercially. He knows that moving through different levels of society is akin to stepping through different rooms in an enormous house, each door leading to a grander environment than the last. He may, of course, settle for the comfort of any room he reaches. Alternatively, he may continue through successive doors to surround himself with even greater fineries and riches."

Simeon threw Barnabas a side glance.

"I am aware of the different levels of wealth, class, and expectation."

"I am sure you are, but imagine if you will, that in each of these rooms there is a party of people, who require that each new arrival makes *them* immediately comfortable with his presence. He must convince *them* of his unquestionable right to be there. They must believe completely and unreservedly that he truly belongs. Note my words well. They must *believe* that he belongs there. Where he comes from, the education he has received, his family history, his wealth, they matter not a jot, but the perception he conveys - that my, boy, is the key. If they believe he belongs - that he is part of the room - then he *does*, he *is*. And whichever room he is about to step into, then that is who he must become."

Simeon was becoming more indignant by the second.

"But, Uncle, you appear to ask me to betray my very being. Should I not be proud of myself? My background? My personality? Because let me tell you, I most certainly am. As, by the way, I thought you were…"

"I am. Very much so."

"And yet you wish me to swap personas like some chameleon

con-man. Perform for people, who think I am not already worthy? You will find I am extremely comfortable in the skin God gave me. This is who I am, and this is who I shall remain!"

Simeon pulled away from the tailor and walked across to gather his belongings, intent on leaving the shop, if only to catch a little air and calm down. Barnabas, however, appeared to ignore the young man's annoyance.

"Walk away if you wish, but do so knowing this. We are all constantly judged by the way we look and the things we do. God might have given you that skin, my boy, and He might very well be able to stare into the deepest recesses of your soul, but the rest of the world simply doesn't care, and few would spare the time even if they could. Rightly or wrongly, they are entangled with their own affairs. They spend time with those whom they feel comfortable with, and those who help them achieve something, while avoiding those who do not or cannot. Yes. It is unfair. Yes. It is harsh. But realistic? Absolutely."

Simeon stopped and looked around, embarrassed once again at his possible overreaction. He gingerly signaled for the tailor to continue, as Barnabas lowered himself into the chair with a soft thud and explained further.

"We must design how we wish to be perceived, and then we must work even harder to continuously recreate and re-evaluate that perception. Improve upon it, adapt it, make it work for us. Mark my words. Perception is reality and how someone perceives you is *their* reality. Whether they are right or wrong is of no concern to them, for they have no reason to question it. Each step of your current journey will take you to new and interesting worlds of opportunity and as every intrepid explorer knows, when one visits strange new lands one must be aware of their customs."

Barnabas held up a sample of cloth, the gentleman to his right nodded and hurried into the cutting rooms located at the rear of the building.

"Have you made yourself aware of Rule Number Five?"

"The one entitled *design your reputation?*"

"It is indeed. Quite so. Quite right! *Design your reputation.* I can best describe it as designing two separate levels of perception. Perception number one, how you want people to think about you when you arrive and perception number two, how you want them to talk about you once you have left."

Simeon smirked. "And how exactly am I supposed to control how people think?"

"You can't control anybody. I thought we had agreed upon that fact yesterday."

"So I should change their perception by taking control of myself?"

"Well, first things first. Let's look at how you want them to think about you when you arrive. We've already discussed your clothes. What about the rest of your general appearance? What else can we ensure looks pristine?"

"Hair? Shoes? Personal grooming?"

"Well done. Yes. Yes. All those things and more. In less time than it takes to burn a short match down to your finger tips, another human being will have made their first impressions of you. After that, eighty percent of everything they think of you is already cast in stone."

"But I can always change their mind at a later point in time."

"Change their mind? *Change their mind?* Well, I've just told you that you only get one chance at a first impression. What if that's the last time you see them? What if your first impression drove them to never see you again, eh? But change their mind you say?" Barnabas smiled. "You will never change a prospective customer's mind, my boy. There is a chance that he might make a new decision if enough reliable evidence comes his way, but to do that he has to want to listen - to hear it - and that requires trust and respect."

"But that's impossible. How can one garner such respect from the very beginning?"

"Well, let me ask you this. What thoughts and feelings would come to mind if your family doctor joined us? How would you treat him, and what would be your perception of his professionalism?"

"Doctor Fides? He is a learned man, who has administered medication and advice to my family since before I was born. He deserves my utmost respect. I would be delighted to be joined by him on any occasion."

"I should hope so. And how often does Doctor Fides call round to administer medication, uninvited, on the off chance that you are unwell?"

"Why, never. If we require his services, we send word. He is far too busy to make random calls. His time is extremely valuable and is spent with those who truly need it."

Simeon positioned himself as straight as he could, while the tailor took measurements from the side of his body, and realized that Barnabas was smiling again at his response.

"More amusement at the expense of my foolish naivety?"

"Not at all. Once again, dear boy, you have seen to the very heart of a rule without even realizing it. Your doctor is indeed an expert at his craft and a continuous student of his art. You seek him out when you need to because he is the one person you trust with the important matters of your family's health. He does not waste his time searching for work. Why should he? People readily bring it to him.

His days are so full that he will only take new patients onto his books when one of his regulars expires. He has a waiting list for his services and his recommendations are rarely questioned. And yet he knows as much about your specialism as you do about his. Do you not deserve the same level of respect from him as he receives from you?"

"But he is a doctor."

"And a fine one, I'm sure. But as you know, our word for doctor originates from the Latin for teacher, eh? Its oldest translation denotes someone, who dedicates their life to learning, spreading knowledge, and sharing solutions. Isn't that exactly what you are doing in your own work? When Doctor Fides is in need of your solution is he able to administer it himself?"

"Well, no. He would require my services."

"Quite so. Quite right! You are both experts in a specific field and yet for some reason you believe that yours is less worthy of respect than his."

"He saves people's lives. It is not comparable."

"Sometimes he does, sometimes he doesn't. He is a human being employed in a noble profession, but that is all. Most men have professions, yet few act like professionals. Let me ask you this. Do you have a waiting list for your services? Do people regularly seek your advice?"

"I wish it was so, but nobody really knows who I am, which is why I continuously present myself to anyone, who will listen or book an appointment."

"Quite. In short, the difference between you and your doctor is that he has a well-designed reputation and you do not."

"A reputation that he has spent over thirty years building. Whereas I have only just begun."

"I didn't say you could purchase a reputation off the shelf of your local grocers. The important thing for now is that you recognize you need to create one. An activity that your competitors are most certainly not planning into their day. Of course, it's going to take time, but it doesn't need to take you anymore than say…twelve months."

"Twelve months? What? By pretending? Creating an untrue perception? You want me to hoodwink people? Become some kind of fraud?"

"I do not wish for you to become anything you are not. Tell me are you a fraud?"

"No. I certainly am not!"

"Ha, thank goodness for that. That would have been a terrible disappointment. Well then, twelve months is more than enough time for an expert of his craft to have started to design a reputation. Once you have focused your efforts upon who your prospective customers are to be, you can start to understand and uncover their problems, their requirements, their issues, and their desires. You can network within these circles and freely offer advice, build trust by delivering a valuable insight mixed with a generous spirit. Too many go into business to make quick money through deception and half-truths, and that is why so many find it difficult to trust a salesman. Once bitten, eh?"

Simeon smiled back at the glint in his uncle's eye, while stretching his arms into a T-shape for the tailor.

"But if I give them too much information what will they need me for?"

"If your doctor told you that you needed immediate surgery could you perform it yourself?"

"No. I would require his experience and expertise."

"Precisely! We're not giving our livelihood away here, my boy. We're simply planting the seeds that will ensure you are called when there is a need. Just like your doctor."

"But what proof can I show to these people? The good doctor has both certificates and a history. I have none of the first and very little of the latter."

"A fine question. Over the course of the twelve months, you will be requesting letters of recommendation from each and every happy customer, building them into a bound presentation for prospects to view as proof of your abilities. Trust me. In a very short time, you will become sought out by those in your network. Initially for your sound advice, but soon after as a provider of service. Few people seek advice about a subject that doesn't require a solution."

"That's really quite well thought out."

"Why, thank you." Barnabas lifted himself from his chair and touched the top of his cane gently onto Simeon's shoulder. "But that's just what they think about you on the way in. How about on the way out?"

"Well, that must surely be based on how I actually act."

"Quite so. Quite right. The way in which you arrive, your punctuality, how you hold yourself in meetings, an ability to keep your promises and constantly over deliver, those qualities and many more are required to ensure that when you leave each appointment, they turn to one another and agree that the experience of being in your company was a good and beneficial one.

Your competition may spend their time trying to snipe and undermine you, however, when someone mentions your competitors you will simply acknowledge them as competition, never uttering a bad word. If their praises are being sung, you find out why, make a mental note and set yourself the target of bettering them. Let your customers and prospects recommend you to each other and let you competition wish they were you. That is our mission."

The company of tailors disappeared quickly through a curtain in the back as a tall, smartly-dressed man walked purposefully across the shop floor and handed Simeon a small, white reservation card with his name and a capital T stamped across the center for reference, before turning towards Barnabas.

"Will that be all, Sir?"

"Yes, I think so, Joseph." replied Barnabas.

"Very good, Sir, please send my regards to the inner chamber."

With that, the small bell rang again as the incredibly well-groomed Joseph held the door for Simeon to leave.

"Don't forget your reservation card for the fifth, Sir. I'm sure you will find that it fits perfectly."

Simeon nodded and stepped into the bright sunlight followed by Barnabas, who took a deep breath of cool, fresh air and leant on his stick.

"I think this is probably the perfect day for a walk round a couple of parks. What do you say?"

"Do we have time?"

"Let us make some time."

With that Barnabas hailed a cab, informed the driver of their destination, and they set off towards Belgravia.

# CHAPTER 11
## The Sixth Rule: Regain the Tenacity of a Child

COMPARED TO THE BUSY STREETS surrounding them, the park felt clean, bright, and alive.

Simeon had spent so much of the week surrounded by the sights and sounds of the largest and most populated city on earth, he had almost forgotten what fresh-cut grass smelled like.

It still surprised him how, only a short walk from the Club, London could be so green and peaceful.

Barnabas brought his stick up to the illustrated map, as they walked through the main gate.

"Today's letter is one of my favorites. Absolutely fabulously hidden. Written into the very fabric of this magnificent park."

"Within the park?"

"Yes. Come. Take a look at the map."

"What am I looking for?"

"The next letter. I've just told you."

"But where should I be looking?"

"Maybe if you opened your eyes you would see it."

"I'm looking for it. How big is it? Is it on an object?"

"No. I've told you. It's written in the park."

"Stop talking in riddles. What does that mean?"

"Look at the shape of the park. The way the trees cut across. Look carefully. What do you see?"

"I see a map of a large, green space. Look. Maybe if you told me where to look, we could go there and I'd find it."

"Sometimes, if you get too close to a subject you can miss what's most important. Humor me. View the map again."

Simeon looked again. From the entrance at which they had entered, the park was wide before them, slowly narrowing until it reached a point at the top. Trees bordered each side and then cut across the middle in a perfectly straight line.

"This is nonsense. I do not know what I am looking for or what it looks like. If it is in the park, let's stop wasting our time and get in there and find it."

Simeon moved off and strode into the park.

"My dear boy, come back here. Let's look together. I'll help."

Simeon stopped, turned and went back to his uncle once again with the face of a petulant infant. He stood staring at the map. His uncle stood behind, resting his hands upon the young man's shoulders to focus his gaze.

"Now, take your time and have a proper look. What do you see?"

"Well, there are trees down either side. The park's quite triangular. There's some more trees going across the middle and… it can't be."

"What is it?"

"The park. My goodness the park is laid out like a capital *A*."

"Is it?" Barnabas smiled, as he stood back and lightly patted Simeon on the back in a congratulatory fashion.

Simeon was giggling like a small boy.

"Look. The whole park. It's planted in the shape of a capital *A*."

"And yet, because you were in such a rush to succeed, you wanted to walk straight past it. Even though I had brought you right up to the solution and indicated its importance."

"I couldn't see it. I just couldn't see it."

"Young man, your problem and the reason so many like you fail, is simply because you allow yourself to give up far too early. No conviction. Tell me. What does Rule Number Six advise us to do?"

"Oh, I know this one. *Regain the tenacity of a child.*"

"Quite so. Quite right. And do you believe you have the tenacity of a child?"

"No. It doesn't make sense. Children? Being tenacious is against their very nature."

Barnabas seemed not to hear and started to walk away, his attention suddenly drawn to a terribly upset young girl, of around six years old, pulling at her mother's shawl.

"Well come on. Keep up, Simeon. We appear to have a fine example unraveling directly before us."

They strolled over a little closer to the drama, and as they approached, the conversation became slowly audible.

By the fence, a balloon salesman was holding twenty, or so, brightly-collored balloons. It was now clear that the little girl wanted one, her mother refusing to make the purchase. However, this young lady was not giving up so easily.

No matter how many times her mother scolded her, she persisted in asking for a large, red balloon. And then after being told that this was not going to happen, demanded to know the exact reasons why. After what felt like an uncomfortable length of time, her argument suddenly switched, and she said, "Well, if I can't have one now, when can I have one?"

Her mother grateful for the respite softened her response slightly, "Soon, luv, soon"

"But when?"

"Not just now."

"When then?"

"Please, Mary, leave me be."

Barnabas smiled and made an observation.

"Look at the way they are dressed. Her mother can probably barely afford to put bread on the table for the next meal. Never mind a folly such as that balloon."

Simeon looked over, trying not to be too obvious.

"Hardly a reason to smile at them, Uncle. Although she certainly doesn't seem to be giving up, does she? You'd think she was poisoned and the balloon has been tied to the antidote."

"Ha. The balloon would probably be some form of antidote for the mother too. If only it could be administered, eh? Fascinatingly resilient the tenacity of a child. Not yet conditioned by society to give up when instructed to do so. She certainly hasn't had her questioning skills knocked out of her just yet either, has she?"

They settled on a bench and Barnabas checked his watch, replaced it, and then banged his stick hard on the dry soil, making Simeon jolt slightly with surprise.

"Take a look at your feet. What do you see?"

Simeon looked down, not quite sure what he was looking for, then lifted his right foot sharply.

"We should move, Uncle. This area is overrun with ants."

"Precisely. Fabulous animals are they not? They know where they are trying to get to, and they know what they are trying to achieve, but what happens when something gets in their way?"

While he was talking, Barnabas picked up a piece of bark, which had fallen onto the bench and placed it directly in the path of the marauding insects. The ants probed this sudden, colossal impediment with their antennae. A few climbed slightly, vying for a better view, trying to see if going over was a possibility. After ruling out that option, they split into two groups and in a regimental Y shape marched round either side of the bark. Barnabas, wide-eyed with excitement, continued to point with his stick.

"Look. You see? They can't give up. It is not in their vocabulary."

"Actually, Uncle, I don't think they have a vocabulary."

"Oh, I wouldn't be so sure. Look at them. Fabulous. In a similar fashion, there can be no success in sales without tenacity. On many occasions your prospects will tell you that they have no need for whatever it is you are trying to sell them. At other times, you will be laughed at and possibly humiliated. The people you will call on as prospects will number in the thousands, and the amount of those who you convert into paying customers will be a tenth, a twentieth, maybe a hundredth of that number.

Seeking those elusive individuals is like mining for rare gems. It will take hard work, patience, and a persistent attitude. To find that rich seam of colorful stones, you will have to chip through dirt and rock. You will have to learn how to hold rubble in your hands and see the fortune inside. You are going to have to regain the tenacity that you had when you were the same age as that little girl over there, while developing the single-mindedness of these ants."

Simeon grimaced.

"But that little girl's persistence is starting to annoy passers-by, embarrass her mother, and has for some time, verged on what can only be described as disrespectful."

Barnabas looked over and gave a wry smile.

"Possibly. She is also probably getting awfully close to being maneuvred out of sight, round the back of that tree, in order for her mother to dispense quite a powerful smack. However, it does not appear to be diminishing her resolve, does it? She has set her mind so solidly on attaining that which she desires, she will scream blue murder until she gets it. Unfortunately, she has no concept of personal wealth or the cost of things in general, and so she cannot appreciate her mother's position or reasoning."

"So, you believe that this rule is about pestering people until they give in?"

"Ha! Good God, no! It's about creating an internal doggedness that doesn't let go of the bone once it's between your teeth. If you honestly know how you help people, then you should become passionate about sharing it, spread the good news, give everyone a chance to share in the solutions that you can provide."

As they continued out towards the perimeter of the park, they approached a preacher standing on a wooden box. His voice booming, arms stretched wide above his head, Bible open in his right hand, passionately sharing his message with a mix of the uninterested, the fanatical, and the embarrassed passersby. Barnabas signaled towards him with his cane.

"From today onward, you will learn how to become evangelical about the many ways you help people. Do you think our preacher friend there wishes to share the good word with others for his own benefit? Do you believe that his passion to share the word of God is of a selfish nature?"

"Well, he is probably doing his best to secure his place in heaven."

"Is he? Do you think so? I reckon he believes that he is already well on his way to paradise, a done deal if you will. In fact, his belief is so passionate that it fills him with the burning desire to share his fabulous news with anyone who will listen. He is concerned that it is us that might be missing out, not him. His faith in a single road to salvation and paradise is so intense, that it would be ungodly not to share the good news with all those who are not aware."

Barnabas stopped for a while, smiling to himself as he listened.

"This is how you must be. You must become as evangelical about your promised outcome as he is about his. You must believe that you, and you alone, have the solution to your prospects problems. Even if they do not recognize those problems themselves. Think upon the numbers I have been sharing with you. Of your competitors, five out of ten will do little more than take their customer's money immorally. A further three out of ten will leave them dissatisfied.

It is your duty to save these prospects from that disappointment. Every potential customer, who misses out on what you have to offer, due to your lack of zeal or passion, every prospect who ends up with an excuse of an alternative from your lackluster competition, should rest heavy on your conscience. You should feel so driven to help the world that it would weigh you down if a single person received anything but the best. Which, of course, is anything but yours."

They walked in a circle, and once again came upon the center of the A-shaped park, stopping to admire London's grandest buildings poking up over the top of the trees. A reminder of how close they were to the city.

"Tell me, Simeon. If you woke before dawn one morning with the formula for a vaccine, which would cure the most ghastly disease currently known to man, releasing millions from an agonizing death, would you roll over and resume sleeping until daylight?"

"No. Of course not. I would jump out of my bed and start to work on some form of production, find the quickest way to save those afflicted."

"Of course you would. And so it must be with the energy you muster for your own work. Get out there and convert the unconverted. Save them all from the charlatans and the nearly-men. Understand why you are different and how you help, recognize your target market, and give them something they might not even realize they are missing."

With that, Barnabas broke away suddenly and made his way over to the balloon salesman, purchased the largest red balloon available, took it to the mother and the, now, crying child.

As he handed it to the little girl, she wiped the tears from her cheeks and looked to her mother for some guidance on whether to accept the gift or not.

Barnabas simply tipped his hat, smiled at them both, and continued along the path, beckoning for Simeon to keep up.

The mother's thank you was drowned by the little girl's shriek of delight, as she skipped away holding her crimson prize tightly by its string.

Barnabas chortled with a shared sense of childish happiness. This small random act of kindness had delivered as much joy to the old man, as it had to its recipient.

"Uncle, I'm not sure that was really the thing to do."

"You know, Simeon, in this world there are those who enjoy giving people balloons and there are those who take great pleasure in popping them. And I wish to be remembered as being firmly in the first party. What do you say?"

Simeon grinned back at him, placing a hand firmly on his uncle's shoulder.

"Of that, there is no doubt, Sir. No doubt whatsoever."

I need a first-class reputation.

I desire for prospects to seek me out, customers to recommend me to their friends, my services to be sought by all who truly need them.

And I wish to be asked for by name.

In the past, I have bargained myself away, believing that price was more important than cost, quality, reliability, or reputation. In the past, I was clearly wrong.

The confidence felt, when dealing with genuine reputation, often outweighs the simplicity of price.

Who would trust a family member's health with a complete

stranger? Who would allow their child to have medication administered by a man dressed as a vagrant?

And who would be willing to put up with less than the desired result, if they could afford to have it done properly?

How we feel about those we give our business to is of vital importance.

What is the true cost of a purchasing decision that goes wrong? All these concerns are appeased, by the introduction of reputation. It is the panacea for those, who lack confidence in their own decisions.

Skeptics are persuaded by a good reputation, for it is an unspoken statement of proof.

It saddens me to note that there will always be con artists and charlatans in the world. Men who aim to fool the public by clothing themselves in the robes of experts, but surely that must give me even more reason to succeed.

In this world of half-jobs and liars, I will prevail.

Therefore, I need to become evangelical about my cause. It is clear to me, now, that I have given up far too easily in the past.

I have discovered fallen trees across my path and have possessed neither the strength to move them nor the patience or tenacity to find an alternative way round. I have simply returned to where I came from, and told myself there had been no other choice.

From today my attitude will change.

Like an ant, I will find my way round any obstacle. Like a child, I will persevere with pinpoint focus. Like the evangelist, I will shine with the light I have been shown, recognize that I have the ultimate solution for all my prospects, nurture that feeling deep within, and repeat the words to myself every day, until there is no doubt in my mind that keeping such good news hidden would be the very worst type of sin.

I will not let those, who cannot recognize how I can be of service, dissuade me from showing them how I can help. And to do this, I will regain the tenacity I had as a child.

I will look the part. I will act the part. I will deliver that which I have promised to deliver.

I will design myself a reputation, in which prospects can place their trust, and customers return to and recommend.

I will design my reputation and my resolve shall be absolute. I shall not give in when I know I can help.

# CHAPTER 12
## A Tour of the Triforium

As they turned the corner out of Creed Lane, St Paul's Cathedral was suddenly in full view. Simeon had to pause for a moment to fully appreciate the scale of the building in front of him. It stood pure, bright, and pristine, against the slate-gray sky.

"Behold the pomp and majesty of genius and endeavor," Barnabas said opening his arms wide and smiling. "Without, within, above and below, the eye is filled with unrestrained delight is it not."

"It is truly spectacular."

"Of that, there is no doubt. However, we have no time for touristic follies. Come, let us go into the house of the Lord, my boy. Our feet are required within the gates."

With that, Barnabas bounded up the cathedral steps with

Simeon doing his best to keep up without breaking into a jog. As they entered through the huge wooden doors, the change of atmosphere was immediately apparent. The hustle and bustle of the busy street outside gave way to a reverent peace and quiet. People talked in hushed tones, while the angelic voices of the choir appeared to seep from the very walls around them, and embrace the entire interior of the cathedral.

"Now then, my dear boy," Barnabas asked as his voice boomed and echoed around the stone walls, "what is this final rule all about then?"

Embarrassed, Simeon answered in a hushed tone.

"It is entitled *listen as if your life depended on it*, which, even taking the previous six into account, all seems a little dramatic. Slightly over the top, don't you think?"

Barnabas looked back in shock.

"No. No. I certainly do not. This most vital rule has purposefully been left till last and I cannot express its importance in the achievement of extreme success."

"But everyone, who has the use of their ears, can listen."

"Quite so. Quite right. But, if that is the case, why is being heard and understood so difficult? I grant you, it may appear that this rule is some level of afterthought, but again this is one of the greatest failures of the nearly-men, always more keen to sell what they have, rather than to find out and help people buy what they actually need."

"I can see why it may need highlighting, but I can't quite see the point of a rule about listening, when we've already had one about questions. Why would anyone go to all the trouble of asking questions, when they had no intention of listening to the answer?"

"Yes. Perplexing is it not? And yet so many do." Barnabas pointed to the sky saying, "Come on. Come with me. I want to show you what real listening can achieve."

Simeon had given up counting after the hundredth step, as they climbed the vast staircase, eventually reaching the very interior of the great dome itself.

"This, my boy, is known as the Whispering Gallery. I want you stand all the way over there," Barnabas said, and raised an arm and indicated loosely with his hand. "On the opposite side, turn to the wall, and whisper any number you like."

Simeon walked round, thinking, "This a rather odd game." Stood as instructed, and quietly whispered, "Six."

He turned to see Barnabas facing him across the divide holding up six fingers. Simeon must have looked slightly puzzled. Barnabas beamed back like an excited child and indicated that he turn round and do it again.

Muttering under his breath, Simeon looked away.

"Right. I'll get you this time. You're cheating me somehow, you old fraud." Once again facing the wall, he whispered as quietly as he could, "Seven thousand five hundred, and ten."

He turned round to see Barnabas first holding up seven fingers, then five, and then ten, and then he bounded round to see his nephew.

"Interesting trick, Uncle. You must show me how to do it one day."

"It is not a trick, dear boy. And just for the record, I am neither a cheat nor a fraud."

"How did you hear that...I mean, don't get me wrong. I..."

"Ha! Don't worry. That's exactly the reaction I was after. It's the dome. It amplifies sound. Fabulous, eh? Come along. There is another staircase I want you to see."

They made their way swiftly back down, before reaching a heavy door, at which Barnabas produced a large key, while warily looking over his shoulder, and then proceeding to open it with a slight nudge of his shoulder.

"Where are we going?" asked Simeon

"The Triforium."

"The what? Are we allowed?"

"I have a key, don't I?"

"Yes, but all this sneaking around. It certainly doesn't feel like we're allowed."

Barnabas gave a huge grin, while locking the door behind them.

"Come on. All will be revealed, as we move through."

Simeon barely had time to take in the shelves, heavy with ancient artifacts lining both sides of the wide corridor, as Barnabas made his way briskly through, before stopping abruptly at the foot of a circular staircase, which swept away high above them towards the top of the south-west tower.

Simeon gazed up. "Ha! Look, Uncle. The way it swirls round. It looks like the cochlea shell from the Club."

"Excellent powers of observation, my boy. A sign that we must be on the right track, eh? I'm sure by now you've started to realize that all these clues are not simple coincidences. Come. There's a final letter to find and a library at the top that I really need you to see."

After another long climb, they reached the top and Barnabas rested on his stick, while gesturing down to where they had begun their ascent.

"Do you see?"

Simeon, rather surprisingly more breathless than the older man next to him, leant over and looked all the way to the foot of the staircase. Down on the floor was another mariner's star reaching out across the cold stone slabs below, with seven silver points, one point gold.

Barnabas put a hand on the ironwork and looked down.

"Ah, the magical number of success!"

"I'm sorry?"

"Eight. The number eight. Have you not noticed how often it keeps popping up?"

"No. I can't say I have."

"Well, by now you should have. I'll have you know that many religions of the world, including our own, believe it represents new beginnings and abundance. For instance, there are eight forms to the Hindu goddess of wealth, and the Buddhists follow something they call the eight right paths. That old star might have multiple interpretations, my boy, but it's there to be recognized by anyone of any creed or color who has the eyes to see it."

"I think you'll find that eight is just a number, Uncle. There is nothing mystical about it. Rather strange though that one point is a different color from the others."

"A little odd, isn't it? Maybe its direction can give us our last letter, eh? Which way does it point?"

"I don't know. There are no other indications. How are we to tell?"

"Well, we are standing in the south-west tower. Surely you can work it out."

Simeon tried to get a bearing on his location, "No. It's no good. I can't do it."

"A lack of tenacity?"

"No. I just don't know where we are. We have been through so many corridors, so many turns."

With a glint in his eye, Barnabas reached into his jacket and produced a small pocket compass.

"This new gizmo might help us. Don't you think?"

"A tiny compass? That's cheating."

"Cheating? Or am I simply using the appropriate tool for the job? Take a look at this and tell me where that gold spike down there is pointing."

Simeon placed the compass on the palm of his hand and steadied himself.

"South. It's pointing south."

"Indeed."

"So, the final letter? Is it *S*?"

Barnabas smiled and brought his hands together with a clap that ricocheted off the circular walls of the tower.

"Quite so. Quite right. Well done, lad. Right. Let's go through this door and make some sense of it all shall we? See if we can put together this jumble of letters, mold them into some version of the truth."

Barnabas returned the compass back to his jacket pocket and stretched his walking-stick arm across Simeon's back to lead him through the heavy, oak door.

# CHAPTER 13
## The Seventh Rule: Listen as if Your Life Depended on It

THE ROOM BEYOND WAS A huge stone chamber lined with bookcases and dark, oak paneling. As the door shut behind them, Simeon immediately felt the atmosphere return to that of serenity, with only the ethereal sound of the cathedral choir singing far below them. Even Barnabas lowered his voice to a hush.

"Welcome to the library," he said, indicating for Simeon to take a seat at a table near the fireplace, while he went to retrieve some books.

As Simeon was waiting, a long-limbed man, with thinning hair and half-moon glasses approached.

"Can I help you, young man?"

"I'm here with my uncle."

"And where is he then?"

"He was here a minute a..." At that moment, Barnabas reappeared with a great stack of books.

"Jeremiah. It's me, Barnabas."

"Barnabas Kreuz. Well, I never. How long has it been, old boy?"

"Too long, Sir, far too long," Barnabas said, putting down the books and shook his friend warmly by the hand. "Jeremiah, may I introduce you to my nephew, Simeon. Simeon, I'd like you to meet a very old friend of mine and the chap in charge of this wonderful collection of knowledge, Jeremiah Mumble."

Simeon stood to shake the librarian's hand as Barnabas continued.

"Do you have those marvelous reference books on Chinese symbols handy, Jeremiah? I don't seem to be able to find them."

"I know exactly where they are. One moment. Which books in particular?"

"Just the one that includes listening."

"Right oh!" And with that Jeremiah scurried across to the other side of the room.

Simeon was confused.

"Why do I need to see the Chinese symbol for listening? I have no idea how to read Chinese. How can it help?"

"All will be revealed, my boy. All will be revealed."

Jeremiah hurried back across the creaking wooden floor and placed a book in front of Simeon, opened at a page, which displayed an illustration of sweeping lines and curves.

It appeared to be a picture of a flag with two stripes across it, blowing to the left on a short pole. To the right hand side, there was a different column of symbols of the same height. A cross sat on a rectangle resting above a line. At the bottom of all this, there appeared to be a cupped hand trying to catch three raindrops.

Jeremiah saw the lost look on Simeon's face and took the liberty to explain.

"The Chinese write in individual symbols like these," said Jeremiah, glancing across the page with a long, thin finger. "Each character is a different word. Most Chinese adults can understand around five thousand of them. Absolutely fascinating don't you think? This character here, in front of you, means to listen." Jeremiah began pointing to each individual symbol in turn, saying, "If you follow it in order it reads - I give you my ears, my eyes, my undivided attention and my heart."

"That's a bit much for listening isn't it?"

"Not at all," Barnabas interjected. "For instance, eye contact is incredibly important, lets the speaker know you're taking an interest and paying attention. As for undivided attention, if you ask me a question then that is what I require, as I give you the answer. And as for the heart, if you listen from the heart, my boy, then you are listening with the utmost respect for the person talking to you. *Speaking* from the heart is simple. Listening wholeheartedly, however, is much, much more difficult and most rare."

Jeremiah polished his glasses with a piece of silver cloth.

"I will give you two a little time to work through the rest together. Just let me know if you need me for anything else. I'll be in my office. Do you have your favorite Latin thesaurus there, Barnabas?"

"Indeed I do, Jeremiah. Good to see you again, my friend."

Barnabas beamed a huge grin and raised his hand to salute a goodbye and then turned back to his nephew.

"You know, most sales people ask questions just for the sake of asking questions. Question after question, on and on. They rarely give the customer a chance to get a word in edgeways."

"It can't really be that hard to listen to someone properly can it?"

"Listening is a discipline. It's all about being present at that moment in time. You have to recognize that what you are trying to do is fully understand the customer before responding. If you don't understand, you ask again."

"Won't that make me look a little stupid?"

"You'll look even more foolish, if you start making recommendations on naive misunderstandings."

"Fair point. Although I think you'll find I already listen when I should, and can take note of anything important as required."

"I'm sure you can. So, how many letters do you have for our mysterious word?"

"Six. $N$, $A$, $V$, $I$, $A$, and $S$."

"*Navias*? Well that's not English. How's your Latin?"

"Latin? Oh I see. *Navias*, er. I think it means ship doesn't it?"

"Indeed it does. So do you think ship is the word that means everything?"

"Hardly. How disappointing. What a waste of time."

"Maybe. Or maybe you're missing a letter?"

"Am I? From where?"

"Well, allegedly, according to you, you're always listening when you should be, taking note as required."

"That's hardly fair. Tell me. What have I missed?"

"Well, here we are, Simeon. If you can remember hearing one more clue, one more letter, your life might very well change. If you can't it won't. The rest of your life depends on it. Having the ability to truly listen doesn't seem so dramatic now does it?"

Simeon was getting frustrated.

"If you can tell me where I was or when I missed it, I will probably remember, but this vagueness isn't helping at all. You've made your point. Now tell me. What have I missed?"

Barnabas looked deadly serious once again.

"It's not my fault you missed it. You weren't listening. That's all there is to it."

"Alright. Alright. I admit I don't always pay attention. There. Is that what you want to hear?"

"No. Not at all. But I do want you to start realizing how far away you are from being able to listen professionally. You listen like an amateur and fool yourself into believing it is enough when it is not."

Simeon held his hands up as if to surrender.

"I'm sorry. I am aware that I have been somewhat arrogant and naive this week, but we're so close. Please tell me. Where were we when I missed it?"

"I'm not really supposed to intervene." Barnabas rubbed his chin. "Listen. If it helps, the letter you are missing was eluded to in the last thing Joseph said to us at the tailors yesterday."

"Thank you, fabulous. Let me think. He asked you to say something to the inner chamber. Isn't that what he said?"

"He did."

"So what's that got to do with the last letter?"

"Nothing. That wasn't the last thing he said."

"I think you'll find it was."

"There you go again. It most certainly wasn't. Look. I don't have all day. What did he say about your reservation on the way out?"

"Nothing. No wait. He said the suit would fit perfectly, and it would be ready on the fifth."

"Close, but that's not actually what he said. Do you have your card?"

"My reservation card?" Simeon reached inside his jacket. "I have it here." He pulled out the small, white rectangle and handed it to his uncle. "There you go."

"I don't want it. It's not mine. What does it say? Apart from your name?"

"Well, it has this *T* on it. Wait, is that it? Is the final letter *T*?"

"What would that spell?"

"*NAVIAST.*"

"Well, that's not a word either. Try to remember exactly what he said."

Simeon's face lit up and he held the card aloft.

"I have it. He said that it was for the fifth and that he was sure I'd find that it fits perfectly."

"Think it through."

"Fit perfectly for the fifth." Simeon grinned with recognition. "*T* is the fifth letter."

Barnabas laughed loudly and clapped his hands together again.

"Well done, lad, well done. So what does that spell?"

"*N, A ,V, I ,T, A ,S. Navitas!*"

"*Navitas!* Precisely! But what does it mean?"

"I think it's Latin. I'm not exactly sure of it's meaning. Is it energy?"

"Of a particular kind. I think we will require that Latin thesaurus that Jeremiah alluded to. Won't we?"

# CHAPTER 14
## An Intriguing Interpretation

S IMEON WAS NOW ENGROSSED in this mysterious word.

"So why *navitas*? Why did all these great men decide to chisel the word *navitas* into the foundations of London?"

"Why indeed. The answer is a simple one, but alludes to a much more intricate puzzle. Tell me. Do you remember the old book from last Sunday evening? The one you found your letter on?"

"The Eighth Book? The Book of Success?"

"Quite so. Quite right. Yes. The Book of Success."

"What about it?"

"Well, on the very first page of that book is a strange and intriguing message that must have been put there many, many years after the book was originally written. We believe it was possibly added sometime in the Middle Ages by one of the chaps, who found the book and brought it back to England."

"What makes you say that?"

"Because the message is in Latin."

"But why would anybody write on such an ancient manuscript?"

"Probably to help those, who came after. You see, whoever it was appears to have tried to condense the entire book into a single phrase. It must have taken them a lifetime."

"Why? What does it say?"

"Ah, therein lies the problem. You see translating is a funny old business. One translator may see one meaning in a passage whereas another may see something completely different. Sentences can be changed completely by the slightest difference, a single word."

"So, what's the gist of this one, then?"

"The first part is easy enough. It translates as: Before any man can taste success he must first possess."

"What? What must he first possess?"

"*Navitas.*"

"Well that should be easy enough. We look it up, find out what it means, and make our way back to the Club with the formula for success before tea."

"If only it were that simple, eh? Unfortunately, *navitas* has become another part of the puzzle, due to the fact that it can be translated in so many different ways."

"Ah, with it being the word that means all things and all that?"

"And all that. Precisely. But this is clearly no way to eat an elephant, eh? Let's get started. What do we have?"

Simeon turned to his pile of books.

"Well, the first translation I have here is for the word energy."

"But, does it fit?"

"Sort of, let's see. Before any man can taste success, he must first possess energy. That makes some sort of sense doesn't it?"

He looked across to his uncle who appeared to be just staring across at him smiling

"Indeed it does, my boy. Energy meaning that with spirit, vigor, and drive. You've got to be driven to become successful. Then again, there are further definitions of energy. It could, of course, refer to enterprise or power. Any of those could be the secret ingredient to success. A fabulous start. A fabulous start. But let's keep going, eh? What others do you have?"

Simeon thumbed through another book.

"This older edition says it could mean sedulity. What's sedulity?"

"Really? Does no one learn anything at school anymore? Sedulity, my boy, to persevere, to be constant in effort. Not unlike the tenacity of a child, eh?"

"Yes, and I suppose that's not a coincidence is it? Hold on, here's another. This one says that it could be translated as zeal."

"Ha, zeal. Fabulous. Fabulous. Referring to one's enthusiasm and passion. Someone who could possibly be described as adopting the positive."

Barnabas smiled and gave a knowing wink. Simeon continued excitedly. He suddenly felt as if he was uncovering some great and ancient mystery.

"Here's another. How about assiduity?"

"Assiduity. Wonderful word, don't you think? Attention, attentiveness, concentration. Listening as if your life depended on it, eh?"

"Ha! I think I see a pattern forming. How about activity?"

"But of course, activity. Movement, motion, actually taking the journey that you set yourself."

"Diligence?"

"Diligence, meticulous, thorough, conscientious. The very way a man designs his reputation."

"Application?"

"Ah yes. Application. Dedication, study, single-mindedness delivered with intense devotion and commitment to a cause. That is how you get organized. That is how you plot your course."

"And finally, this one says ardor? Ardor? That's a little off track isn't it?"

"Do you think? Ardor, meaning intense desire or love."

Simeon gave a little sneer. "Not really what we're after then."

"So you might think, but you must have realized by now that when one really cares, really tries to help, the other party recognizes the fact and, therefore, easily sees the logic in working together for the greater good, for the mutual benefit of both."

Simeon slapped his right palm onto his thigh.

"The transference of feeling."

"Precisely. So let us see what we have when we put it all together then." Barnabas cleared his throat before starting the passage again.

"Before any man can taste success, he must first possess energy and drive, together with tenacity and the ability to truly concentrate. He must possess enthusiasm and a passion for his work, continuously moving himself forward, while remaining meticulous and conscientious in all things. Finally, he must possess a single-minded, focused vision to aid in achieving his ultimate goal, seeking out those who need his help, and then seeking to help everyone he finds."

The young man sat back in his chair considering. A word that encompassed his entire week. A single word that could describe all the rules he must incorporate into every aspect of his life to ensure that he became successful.

Barnabas smiled.

"Amazing what you can find in a book, eh?"

"Uncle, to be fair, I think it's quite amazing where you find your books."

Barnabas laughed a loud and joyful laugh and leant forward on the table.

"You, my boy, have been well worth my time and effort. Thank you for giving me your week. It has been an absolute joy."

"No, Uncle. Thank you. It's been...I don't know...it's been illuminating."

"It has been my pleasure, is what it has been." Barnabas looked at his nephew with a proud glint in his eye and then gave that big, friendly smile that Simeon had seen so often. "Now, let's get back to the Club for dinner. It's Friday and that means a perfectly good menu of brain food to discuss navitas over, don't you think?"

"It sounds perfect, Uncle. Absolutely perfect."

*Journal Entry*
*Friday, 9th September 1887*

In the past, I have all too often listened without hearing, asking questions when I had no intention of hearing the answer or understand my customer's requirements. Instead, I was just asking to get myself towards the next question and the next, to lead me towards my close, forever trying to make my sale.

Worse, whilst people have answered questions, I have only heard my own voice thinking of the next question. I was so sure that I knew what they needed and what I wanted to sell them that I never stopped long enough to find out what it was they wanted to buy.

Indeed, if it hadn't been for the kindness of my uncle, I would have missed an incredibly important part of this most incredibly important puzzle, to the point that I would not have had the word at all. Everything would have been for nothing just because I simply didn't listen.

When I asked my uncle during dinner, what he thought the most important lesson of the week was, he simply answered that I should become happier at what I do and leave others happier than before they'd met me.

Finding happiness by delivering it. That was most certainly a thought I did not arrive here with.

So with a heavy heart, I leave early in the morning. This week has been spectacular, although I also leave excited at the opportunity to use all that I have learnt and start afresh.

From now on, I must prove to everyone here that I deserve my membership of The Extremely Successful Salesman's Club.

# CHAPTER 15
## We Meet Again In Exactly One Year

As the farms and fields bobbled past the carriage window throughout his journey back home, Simeon thought long and hard about the lessons learnt during this most eventful of weeks. Reaching for his journal, he made copious notes, breathing life into ideas, and creating an abundance of opportunities for the first time.

After about an hour, he stopped abruptly, realizing he had completely lost track of time. Closing his journal, he looked out at the passing view, to work out where he was and he tried to get an indication of how much further he had left to travel.

Reaching into his jacket for his watch, he found Barnabas's farewell letter, and decided that the time at present was of no real consequence, he would arrive when he arrived.

Instead of worrying about the time, he would read his uncle's words again until committing each one to memory.

*Dear Simeon,*

Thank you for being such a wonderful student over this past week. You really were the most perfect apprentice I could have wished for.

I know that I tested both your character and patience, during our time together. Forgive me if you found my methods hard at times. My intention was, only, ever to help you see the light shining brightly in front, and inside, of you.

From the moment you decided to take this journey, your life started to change. Just as it did for me many years ago.

I foresee a fabulous future stretching out in front of you. However, you will do well to remember that destiny and fate are of one's own making, and riches and happiness are rarely found at the end of an easily-traversed path.

The choices you make from this day forward will lead you, step by step, to the future you deserve. Note well my words, for what you deserve will be down to you, and you alone.

Finally, try to think of our seven rules more as good habits than commandments. Treat them as such and you will find that they will integrate into your life with ease.

Adopt the positive in everything you do, for there will always be positivity there to find, if that is what you seek.

Embrace the fundamentals like the closest of friends, for they will be the foundation of your future success.

Plot each and every course with as much detail as it warrants, to ensure you give yourself the very best chance for a successful outcome, and then make sure you take the journey without fear, but with as much enthusiasm and vigor as you can muster.

Spend your time designing the greatest reputation a man could possess. Make sure everyone, who works with you or for you, feels the need to tell others about the incredible experience.

Regain the tenacity of a child. Tell your good news as an evangelist would. Do so with a passion driven by a need to help and solve problems that some people didn't even know they had.

And finally, Nephew, listen to people from your heart, as if your life depended on it, and you will find that in turn people will listen to you with all of theirs.

Spend your next few months devoted to these teachings and prepare yourself to meet me again at the Club on the same date in one year's time, as our original appointment, to assess your successes and see if you are ready to step up to the next level.

I am confident you will be.

Once you have proven that the seven rules have been put to good use, you will be given the chance to move from neophyte to journeyman. You will be introduced to the five truths, and that, my dear Simeon, is a week I am thoroughly looking forward to spending with you.

Until then, I wish you every success and happiness.


Best Regards

*Barnabas Kreuz*

Simeon rested his forehead against the carriage window.

"One year to change my life. Well, if I can do that much in a week, a year should be a doddle," he thought. He smiled folding his uncle's letter, replacing it back into the inside of his jacket, while deciding who was going to be his first appointment on Monday morning.

And that's when the journey truly began.

# The Extremely Successful Salesman's Club

Keep up to date with all ESS Club news, success tips and free exercise templates with the quarterly Club newsletter.

Visit the official website at **www.TheESSClub.com** to find out more.

## About the Author

Chris Murray has become prominent as an inspirational speaker, author and sales training coach, delivering workshops and keynote speeches that challenge teams to re-examine what it means to be '*in sales*' and requiring them to stand back and view the whole experience from a refreshingly different angle.

Chris is also founder and Managing Director of Varda Kreuz, one of the UK's most innovative training and development organisations.